Arthur Samuel Peake
1865-1929

From the portrait by A. T. Nowell

ARTHUR SAMUEL PEAKE: 1865–1929

[Frontispiece

Arthur Samuel Peake
1865-1929

ESSAYS IN COMMEMORATION

by

ELSIE CANN	T. W. MANSON
W. E. FARNDALE	H. G. MEECHAM
ALEXANDER B. HILLIS	A. VICTOR MURRAY
W. F. LOFTHOUSE	LESLIE S. PEAKE
JOHN T. WILKINSON	

and Selections from his Writings

Edited by
JOHN T. WILKINSON

WIPF & STOCK · Eugene, Oregon

Wipf and Stock Publishers
199 W 8th Ave, Suite 3
Eugene, OR 97401

Arthur Samuel Peake 1865 - 1929
Essays in Commemoration
By Wilkinson, John T.
Copyright©1958 Methodist Publishing - Epworth Press
ISBN 13: 978-1-5326-0288-7
Publication date 7/15/2016
Previously published by Epworth Press, 1958

Every effort has been made to trace the current copyright owner of this publication but without success. If you have any information or interest in the copyright, please contact the publishers.

CONTENTS

FOREWORD 7

BIOGRAPHICAL SKETCH 9

PART I

IN COMMEMORATION

1 ARTHUR SAMUEL PEAKE: A RETROSPECT 15
by H. G. Meecham, M.A., D.D., Ph.D.
Formerly Principal of Hartley Victoria College, Manchester

2 OXFORD DAYS 22
by W. F. Lofthouse, M.A., D.D.
Formerly Principal of Handsworth College, Birmingham

3 MANCHESTER UNIVERSITY 34
by T. W. Manson, M.A., D.Litt., D.D., F.B.A.
Rylands Professor of Biblical Criticism and Exegesis in the University of Manchester

4 AUTHOR AND EDITOR 37
by A. Victor Murray, M.A., B.D., B.Litt.
President of Cheshunt College, Cambridge

5 ECUMENICAL CHURCHMAN 42
by John T. Wilkinson, M.A., B.D., F.R.Hist.S.
Principal of Hartley Victoria College, Manchester

6 A LAYMAN'S TRIBUTE 53
by Alexander B. Hillis
Sometime Treasurer of Hartley Victoria College, Manchester

7 IMPRESSIONS OF AN EARLY STUDENT 58
by W. E. Farndale, D.D.
President of the Methodist Conference 1947

8 IN THE STUDY 65
  by Elsie Cann
  Private Secretary 1904–29

9 IN THE FAMILY CIRCLE 73
  by Leslie S. Peake, M.A., B.Litt.
  Minister of the Methodist Church, St. Ives

PART II

EXCERPTS FROM THE WRITINGS OF A. S. PEAKE

CRITICAL

1 THE LEGITIMACY AND NECESSITY OF BIBLICAL CRITICISM 83
2 THE PERMANENT RESULTS OF BIBLICAL CRITICISM 87
3 HISTORY AS A CHANNEL OF REVELATION 91

BIBLICAL

4 THE TEACHING OF JEREMIAH 97
5 THE TEACHING OF THE EPISTLE TO THE HEBREWS 111

THEOLOGICAL

6 THE QUINTESSENCE OF PAULINISM 116

ECCLESIASTICAL

7 THE REUNION OF THE CHRISTIAN CHURCHES 143

APPENDIX: SELECT BIBLIOGRAPHY 161

FOREWORD

FOLLOWING the twenty-fifth Anniversary of the death of Dr A. S. Peake, those who were once his students—'Peake's men' as they delighted to own themselves—strongly desired that some tangible memorial should be instituted. Two things were decided upon. First, the establishment of an annual Lectureship, to be called the 'A. S. Peake Memorial Lecture', for which a generous Fund has been raised, this annual Lecture to be given by a notable scholar in the realm of biblical interpretation. The Inaugural Lecture was given in 1956. A literary memorial was also decided upon, hence this present volume. The work has assumed larger proportions than was originally intended, but it has been thought well that Peake should speak to this present generation through his own writings; therefore representative extracts form the second part of this book. The things for which Peake stood are still in need of constant emphasis.

In sending forth this book our only desire is that it may help to secure a still deeper recognition of Peake as one of the great masters of biblical interpretation for all intelligent readers of Holy Scripture in this and coming generations.

Our thanks are due to the following for permission to reprint selections from Peake's writings:

To Messrs Hodder & Stoughton for excerpts from *The Bible: its Origin, Significance and Abiding Worth* and *The Nature of Scripture;*

to Messrs Thos. Nelson & Sons Ltd for sections from *Jeremiah* and *Hebrews* in The Century Bible series;

to the Trustees of John Rylands Library, Manchester, for *The Quintessence of Paulinism;*

to the National Free Church Federal Council for the Presidential Address (1928).

In addition our thanks are due to Miss Alice Stockdale for the typing of the manuscript.

JOHN T. WILKINSON

ARTHUR SAMUEL PEAKE,
M.A., Hon.D.D. (Oxon), Hon.D.D. (Aberdeen)

A BIOGRAPHICAL SKETCH

ARTHUR SAMUEL PEAKE was born on 24th November 1865 at Leek in Staffordshire. The family originated in that county and was closely associated with Methodism from the days of its founder. His paternal grandfather was converted under the Primitive Methodists, and became a valued local preacher. Two of his sons entered the Primitive Methodist ministry, and the younger of these, the Rev. Samuel Peake, the father of Arthur, though a man of somewhat stern temperament, was deeply religious and a fervent evangelist. Peake's mother, although she belonged to an Anglican background, also experienced conversion under the Primitive Methodists. She was a woman of beautiful character, a true helper of her husband, but toiling beyond her strength, she died when her son was but ten years old. He ever regarded her with the deepest affection and spoke of her profound influence; some who knew both declared that they saw the saintliness of the mother mirrored in the son.

Educated at the Grammar Schools of Ludlow, Stratford-on-Avon, and the King Henry VIII school at Coventry, Peake went in 1883 to Oxford with a Close Scholarship from St John's College and a School Exhibition from Coventry. In 1885 he took a Third in Classical Moderations. Two years later he was elected Casberd Scholar at St John's College, and in that year took a First Class in the Honours School of Theology. In 1889 he was elected Denyer and Johnson Scholar—the most valuable prize that Oxford had to offer—and the following year he gained the University Prize for the Ellerton Essay on 'The Relation of Montanism to the Doctrine and Discipline of the Catholic Church'.

In the same year he was appointed Lecturer at Mansfield College, Oxford, where he taught Hebrew and lectured on Old Testament History and Theology and Patristic Texts. In October of that year he was elected to a Theological Fellowship at Merton College—the first Nonconformist layman to be elected to the Fellowship.

During these years he was successively President of the St John's Essay Society, the St Hilary Society, and the Milton Society in the University.

Whilst at Oxford Peake came under the stimulating influence of five great scholars, Cheyne, Driver, Sanday, Fairbairn, and Hatch, and from all these he gained an insight into the historical approach to the study of the Bible, a field in which in after years he was eminently to excel. During this period also he became a local preacher and a teacher in the Sunday-school, the latter foreshadowing his later campaigns for Sunday-school reform in which he was a pioneer.

In 1892 Peake was appointed tutor at Hartley College, Manchester, the theological college associated with the training of the Primitive Methodist ministry. Thus began his outstanding contribution to Primitive Methodism. This opening was made possible by the foresight of Mr (afterwards Sir) William P. Hartley, who had met Peake in Oxford, and who had a deep concern for matters of ministerial education. Naturally Principal Fairbairn of Mansfield College was anxious to retain Peake, but with fine insight he perceived that it was Peake's duty to answer the call of his own Church. He wrote to Peake: 'It seems to me as if you had been specially raised up and trained for the very work . . . and you are in many ways the only person that can do the work.' Thus began a college tutorship of thirty-seven years. Alongside this tremendous service in Manchester, he became lecturer at the Lancashire Independent College (1895–1912) and for the latter part of that period also at the United Methodist College.

In 1904 he was appointed to be the first Rylands Professor of Biblical Criticism and Exegesis in the University of Manchester, an office which he held to the end of his life, and which opened to him a wider scope and gave him an assured place in the theological world. Thus he became the chief formative influence in the newly-formed Faculty of Theology and was its first Dean (1904–8). In 1905 he edited the *Inaugural Lectures* for the Faculty. In 1925 he became Pro-Vice-Chancellor of the University.

Peake's literary output was enormous, both in books and countless articles and reviews. For a considerable period he continued a correspondence column in the pages of the *Primitive Methodist Leader*, by which a vast amount of biblical and theological information was disseminated, for he believed that he had a vocation to mediate the fruits of scholarship to ordinary folk. In connexion with the John Rylands Library, Manchester, he fulfilled a great service. He was made a member of the Council of Governors in 1899 and eventually succeeded to the Chairmanship of that body. Other members of that council were often astonished at the extraordinary width of his knowledge of literature in many fields other than his own.

In 1919 he became Editor of the *Holborn Review*, the quarterly journal of the Primitive Methodist Church, and this position he retained until his death. He raised it to a very high standard, and not the least of his contributions were his Editorial Notes, frequently reminiscent of scholars of world-wide reputation whom he had known intimately. After his death many of these Notes were gathered together by the late Dr Wilbert F. Howard in a volume entitled *Recollections and Appreciations*. Also in 1919 was issued *Peake's Commentary of the Bible*, the work by which he will perhaps be longest remembered. It was an outstanding editorial achievement. In 1925 at the request of the Society for Old Testament Study (of which he was an originator and in 1924 the President) he edited *The People and the Book*. In the same year under his joint-editorship with Dr Parsons came *An Outline of Christianity* in four volumes.

As a Church leader Peake was outstanding. In 1918 he became a member of the Methodist Union Committee; in 1922 he began to attend the Conferences at Lambeth following the famous 'Lambeth Appeal'; in 1928 he was elected President of the National Free Church Council. He was also a valued member of the Federal Council of the Free Churches, the importance of which in matters of reunion he greatly regarded. During these significant years of ecumenical development he was everywhere recognized as a true guide.

His scholarship inevitably won recognition. In 1906 he received the honorary degree of D.D. from the University of Aberdeen, and in 1920 the D.D. of his own University of Oxford, being the first Nonconformist layman to be given this distinction.

Peake's knowledge of all biblical problems was wide and thorough, but he always retained a special interest in the Old Testament. Early in life he had grasped the importance of the critical study of the Bible, and he never wavered in affirming its value both for sound theology and religious experience. Perhaps one of his greatest achievements was the mediation of this new approach to a vast number of ordinary people. He won a growing influence in his own community, to whom both the letter and authority of the Scriptures were counted as very sacred, and it was the combination of scholarship and piety in Peake that gave him so great an influence with his students. Moreover he believed that the growth of knowledge in this field would produce eventually a closer *rapprochement* between the various Churches of Christendom. Surveying his life, one who knew him well wrote the following shortly after his death:

Perhaps it was Peake's greatest service, not merely to his own communion but to the whole religious life of England that he helped to save us from a fundamental controversy such as that which had devastated large sections of the Church in America. He knew the facts which modern study of the Bible had brought to light. He knew them and was frank and fearless in telling them, but he was also a simple and consistent believer in Jesus, and he let that be seen too; therefore men who could not always follow him were ready to trust him, and let him go his own way. If the Free Churches of England have been able without disaster to navigate the broken waters of the last thirty years, it is largely to the wisdom and patience of trusty and trusted pilots like Arthur Samuel Peake that they owe it.'

He died on 19th August 1929 in his sixty-fourth year.

PART I
ESSAYS IN COMMEMORATION

ARTHUR SAMUEL PEAKE
A RETROSPECT[1]

IT is fitting that this Memorial Service should be held at this time and in this place. A quarter of a century ago Arthur Samuel Peake passed from our midst. It was too early then to assess the value of his labours. The lapse of the years enables us to see the man and his work in true perspective. And in what more appropriate place could this service be held than this college where Peake taught for thirty-seven years, and this chapel where men came to know him as saint no less than scholar?

To many of you present tonight Peake is but a name. To some of us who were privileged to be his pupils and friends he is still a living presence. We naturally think of him first as a biblical scholar and theologian, in particular as a consummate exegete of Holy Scripture. Of his eminence in the realm of learning there can be no question. His death evoked in the Press tributes of unstinted admiration. The stages of Peake's academic career, culminating in a theological fellowship at Merton and a lectureship at Mansfield College, Oxford, mark a triumphal progress. Oxford set his mental mould. There he came under the influence of Sanday and especially Fairbairn, his great friend and teacher. His arrival at Oxford was timely. The historic method of biblical interpretation had emerged under brilliant tutelage. It was destined to find in Peake a skilled popular exponent. To Oxford he owed an incalculable debt. It is eloquent of his obedience to what he felt was a divine call that he left that home of ancient culture to guide the new development in ministerial training in this college and city. Nothing in later life gave him greater pleasure than the conferment of the honorary doctorate in divinity of Oxford University.

What were the contributory factors in a career of such distinction? In the first place there was the native quality of his mind. This revealed itself to our astonishment and admiration again and again in the Lecture Room as in his published work. Insight into

[1] An Address delivered at a Commemoration Service held at Hartley Victoria College, Manchester, on 11th November 1954.

a writer's meaning, a wonderful memory, judicial ability to marshal and weigh all available evidence, the power to form a reasoned conclusion, lucidity of thought expressing itself in an easy and attractive literary style—all these and more were in his possession. With these I would mention a certain magnanimity of spirit that manifested itself in wide sympathies. It is not given to every man to present fairly and persuasively a point of view that he cannot share. But in his little book *Prisoners of Hope* (1918) Peake made a moving plea for toleration of the scruples of the conscientious objector at a time when the fever of war made dispassionate judgement more difficult and rare. Two gifts were outstanding. Peake was able to survey as a whole all the relevant facts and to handle each with meticulous accuracy in detail. The material was always at ready command. His exactness in the minutiae was remarkable. In this blend of comprehensiveness and precision we see the hall-mark of the scholar. To all this was added an unflinching regard for truth and a tireless industry that was the wonder of all his friends.

It is not to be supposed, however, that his mind was without its limitations. His friend and colleague, James Hope Moulton, frequently confessed his own inability to appreciate and even understand philosophical reasoning; Peake for his part disliked mathematics. He rejected entirely the mathematical axiom: 'Never put anything down that you cannot prove.' A former Principal of this college who began his academic career as a Cambridge mathematician turned later to Semitics; Peake was wont to refer to him as 'a brand plucked from the burning'!

Peake's greatness as a theologian, however, had a deeper source than natural endowment. He was a sound interpreter of Holy Scripture because he was a great Christian. In no one has the adage been more fitly fulfilled: 'The heart makes the theologian.' The religious quality of his mind and heart was unmistakable. A distinguished Methodist scholar has written: 'I find it a means of grace to read his works, as well as a literary treat—his character seems to shine through.' Who of us that heard them can forget the spiritual uplift of his addresses in this Chapel, or his prayers in some after-service prayer meeting? Peake's insight into what was for him the central doctrine of Paulinism, the mystical union of the believer with Christ, was the reflex of his own rich experience of fellowship with his Lord. His three booklets written as 'Aids to the devotional study of the Scripture' reveal the depth and reality of his religious life. A son of the manse, he was never ordained; but no name in the lay ranks of Methodism is held in higher honour.

Peake's first book, *A Guide to Biblical Study* (1897), was typical. He excelled in both parts of the field. For the Old Testament we have his commentaries on Job and Jeremiah, his Hartley Lecture, *The Problem of Suffering in the Old Testament* (1904), and the posthumous volume, *The Servant of Yahweh and Other Lectures* (1931), not to name numerous articles and lectures. He was elected President of the Society for Old Testament Study in 1924. But with equal facility he handled the New Testament also. We need only mention his *Critical Introduction*, commentaries on *Hebrews* and *Colossians*, study of the *Apocalypse*, and lectures on Paul. Practically all his written output centred in expositions of Scripture, with occasional excursions into literary and biographical studies. He seemed to be familiar with all the relevant literature of his subject. His students were constantly impressed with his cognizance of what was happening in fields other than his own. William Temple, then Bishop of Manchester, has recorded how Peake as Chairman of the Book Committee of the John Rylands Library would frequently astonish his fellow-members by his acquaintance with the issue of new books in various countries.

I must mention here Peake's fine editorial gifts. The one-volume *Commentary* rightly bears his name. Apart from his own large contributions (eleven in all, covering all sections of the work) it shows everywhere his hand at work in, for example, the additional notes, the revised book lists, and an occasional gentle *caveat!* In the same class stands his editorship of *The People and the Book*, of *The Holborn Review*, and (along with the then Bishop of Middleton) of *An Outline of Christianity*. Peake's reviews in particular were notable. For some ten years he contributed to *The Holborn Review* editorial sketches of great scholars most of whom he knew in person. In these causeries, collected and edited by Wilbert F. Howard in *Recollections and Appreciations by A. S. Peake* (1938), we have valuable critical estimates of the work of some of the leading scholars in all lands.

Several features of his biblical work call for notice. In the Old Testament Peake took what was then an advanced position. In the New he was more conservative. But in respect of both he was convinced that 'many assured results have been reached which the future is not likely to reverse'. Much of his published material was intended primarily for student and preacher. But he had a larger constituency in view. Peake felt himself called to the task of popularization. He did not disdain the function of the middle man. Whilst capable of work of the severest scientific method and value, and able to keep abreast of technical investigations, he nevertheless laid upon himself the duty of mediating the findings of modern biblical research in readable and interesting form.

Perhaps this aim explains the width of his interests. Perhaps also it was the fruit of the broad humanistic culture on which his biblical learning was based. Through such books as *Christianity, its Nature and its Truth* (which reached its sixth impression in six months and was translated into Chinese), *The Bible, its Origin, its Significance and its Abiding Worth*, *The Nature of Scripture*, etc., he became 'guide, philosopher and friend' to a multitude of readers. To the same end he gave himself freely to public lectures and conferences. In all of these he made luminous the real character of the Book as the record of God's gradual self-revelation in history and experience, culminating in His disclosure 'in a Son'.

How far did he succeed in broadcasting the new view? F. C. Burkitt, speaking at the twenty-fifth celebration of the Faculty of Theology in the University of Manchester, expressed his judgement that it was largely due to Peake's work and influence that this country had been spared the odium of a public Fundamentalist controversy. He himself came through by no means unscathed. Were it not painful to reflect on the lack of charity that can prevail in religious circles, it would be amusing to recall some of the opprobrious epithets by which he was described for the edification of the faithful. That, in the words of a religious periodical, he was 'doing Satan's work' was among the mildest accusations brought against him. Of the quality and importance of his work in biblical exposition the ministry and educated laity in the main had no doubt. For nearly forty years he laid his spell on successive generations of students and preachers. True, his conclusions were often guarded. His personal opinion was sometimes withheld, whilst the views of others were always fully—and fairly—expounded. The reason for this reserve lay not in lack of conviction, still less in courage to declare it. It was due to respect for the intellectual development of his men. He would not have them echo views that they had not made their own.

He used to say that all he could do was to give us the right point of view. It was an inestimable boon. To present a cut-and-dried scheme of doctrine is not the prime duty of a theological teacher. Peake rendered a far greater service. He opened our eyes to the rich and spacious fields of biblical knowledge. He inspired us with something of his own reverence and love for the Scriptures. He set our feet upon ground on which we felt we could firmly stand—the progressive revelation of God to men, the uniqueness of Jesus as Lord and Saviour, the power and wonder of the Gospel. In the light and strength of all this he sent us forth to preach.

In Hartley College, where his major work was done, he built up a curriculum which in range and balance was second to none. Immediately on his appointment as tutor he instituted six distinct biblical courses, three on the Old and three on the New Testament. The College curriculum has remained since then considerably weighted on the biblical side. Yet with all his concern for the centrality of scriptural studies in ministerial training, he was alive to the relevance of wider disciplines. Through his initiative Professor Atkinson Lee was appointed to the staff to develop the philosophical side of the curriculum, to the immeasurable gain of generations of students. To the Primitive Methodist Church in general he rendered this great service, that he piloted the vessel through what might easily have become a stormy sea. That not a few were disquieted was inevitable. But what saved the Church from conflict and defection was the confidence felt in this great teacher, a confidence based not merely on his intellectual eminence, but far more on his unwavering loyalty to the evangelical Faith. He was trusted because of his genuine piety. Suspicion dissolved before his passionate devotion to Christ. To Peake it was given to save his Church from a crude obscurantism, and to show how compatible is a modern outlook with evangelical fidelity. Steadily men were led to view wider horizons. It is no surprise that many Primitive Methodist ministers habitually fed on the strong meat of theological reading and thinking. The Presidential address that Peake gave from the Chair of the National Free Church Council was typical of the man. It was memorable for its steadfast loyalty to the fundamentals of the Gospel in general, and to the

Protestant witness in particular, and was delivered, as most of his public utterances were, without a note.

Today there is a marked revival of biblical theology. Nothing would gladden Peake's heart more. For primarily he was an interpreter of Scripture. For him criticism was secondary and ancillary; but it was no less necessary. If, as seems likely in certain quarters, this recent emphasis implies a disparagement of or even a divorce from the critical labours of thirty or forty years ago, it is an ominous sign. No theology can hope to prevail that is not built four-square on the foundations laid by sane and reverent biblical criticism. The preparatory disciplines of linguistic and textual study, what Harnack called 'real scavenger's labour', are still necessary if theology is to be securely based. Was it not Fairbairn who said, 'He who would be a theologian must first be a philologian'?

If it is permissible to specify any one part of our debt to Peake we must name his exposition of Paul's mind and thought. Here in Vernon Bartlet's judgement he most showed originality. For Peake Paul was the great figure of the New as Jeremiah was of the Old dispensation. With deep insight Peake portrays Paul's sense of utter failure to meet the rigorous demands of the Jewish Law and his experience of the release and power he found through the redeeming grace of God in Christ. We sorrow that he was not spared to give to the world a complete treatise of Pauline theology. His three Rylands Lectures (*The Quintessence of Paulinism; Paul the Apostle: his Personality and Achievement; Paul and the Jewish Christians*) serve to remind us how heavy is our deprivation. We think too of the unfinished work on the history of the religion of Israel, and the projected *International Critical Commentary* on Isaiah 40–66. But we would not dwell on loss. Rather would we thankfully acknowledge how rich we have been made by this devoted life.

Peake's work in the University of Manchester is well known. Along with others he took a leading part in the foundation of a Faculty of Theology. He became its first Rylands Professor of Biblical Exegesis, a position he held till the time of his death. He served also as Pro-Vice-Chancellor of the University. For some years he lectured in the Lancashire Independent and the United Methodist Colleges. Of Peake's deep interest in the wider ecclesiastical life of his time there is abundant evidence. He rejoiced in every movement toward closer fellowship among the Churches, taking his part in conversations at Lambeth. The cause of Methodist Union found in him a strong supporter. His patient understanding in Committee and his skilful advocacy in Conference were invaluable in the early critical stages.

Of the man it is not easy to speak. So many memories come to mind. At the lecture desk he was quiet and dignified, absorbed in his immediate task, but quick to detect frivolity or inattention. He was gentle, but never weak; always patient, except with slackness or pretence. No student could take undue liberties. A caustic remark quietly made was more than sufficient to discomfit the offender. What a rich play of humour lit up his lectures and enlivened his table-talk! He had a seemingly inexhaustible stock of stories upon which he could draw at will to the gaiety of the occasion. How he relished to tell anecdotes against himself! Chess and the reading of detective stories seem to have been his only recreations.

Above all there remains the memory of his genuine goodness, his many unrecorded acts of kindness, his truly catholic outlook and hope, his loyalty to his own Church and people. It was not given to him to attain length of life; but how full and rich his days! Being dead, Arthur Samuel Peake still speaks in the printed page, in the abiding inspiration of many ministers of the Word who were privileged to sit at his feet, and most of all in the influence of a consecrated life. Words which he himself loved to quote may well stand as his memorial:

Not till the hours of light return,
All we have built do we discern.

H. G. MEECHAM

OXFORD DAYS

THE chapters of this book present various aspects in the life of a great man, any one of which would afford material for a complete volume. The few pages entrusted to me are in no sense intended to serve as a biographical sketch. That would need more space and another pen than mine. It would call for the knowledge of papers and letters to which I have no access. But a man's life is something more than a catalogue of the events which have filled his career. And the few who can remember Arthur S. Peake's early years at Oxford may be forgiven if they hold that something entered into his life there which, perhaps unconsciously to him or to others, informed the aims which he so conspicuously fulfilled, and the emotions which glowed like half-concealed fires beneath all he said and wrote. Few able and receptive men who would 'both gladly learn and gladly teach' have lived for some years in a University without showing the signs of its effect on them.

Peake was never one who would naturally be called an Oxford man. Indeed those who knew him would sometimes suspect that, while studiously courteous to his *alma mater*, he was determined to be free of her parental control. If he was in any sense anchored to an intellectual centre, it was Manchester, not Oxford. But when we try to make our way—always a somewhat perilous proceeding—to the remoter springs of a man's activity, we must be prepared for what our present-day psychologists call ambivalence. Avoidance and approach often lie near to one another in the untrodden ways of a man's thinking. And the end is at times reached when the traveller imagines that for part of his journey at least he has been moving away from it.

I am far from asserting that an advance of this enigmatical nature would serve for a map of Peake's intellectual life. I suspect that if anyone had made the suggestion to him he would have treated it as a joke. What I wish to make clear in the following pages is that the ten years which he spent in Oxford, to be precise from 1883 when he entered St John's College as a scholar, to 1892 when he left his chair at Mansfield for Hartley College in Manchester, gave him something which proved of increasing importance in the thirty-seven years which followed, and is essential to a true estimate of his work. Otherwise they would hardly be worth recalling.

This is not the place to attempt to reconstruct the Oxford that Peake found when he went up. It was still the sweet city of dreaming spires, the home of lost causes. But a change had been beginning to creep into the atmosphere that had brooded there for centuries. Outwardly the city was very much what it had been for the last hundred years and more, save for the railway, which had been kept at a discreet distance, and some new buildings, whose appearance had been criticized by some and ridiculed by others. Motors were unknown, and so, in the early eighties, were bicycles; a single horse-tram offered comfort to labouring pedestrians; and that new creation, the married don, who wanted to reach his house far in the country (a mile and a half or so from the centre of the town) had to use, like everyone else who wanted to get anywhere, his feet. But the married don was himself a portent. From her beginning, Oxford had been the abode of celibacy. Whatever the feelings of the undergraduates as they read their Horace or Ovid, the senior common-rooms were filled with sober elderly men, to whom all change was a turbulent thing, to be resisted with whatever weapons, by no means contemptible, they could wield.

Still, resistance had not always been successful. A university commission had abolished a number of privileges and sinecures. Women had been admitted to the lecture-room (under strict chaperonage) but not to membership of the University. The married dons brought their geniality and family life; the wit and eccentricity of the older common-rooms faded away. In 1871 fell what many thought the most serious blow of all: the doors of the University were thrown open to others than the members of the Anglican Church. In politics the University remained as a whole staunchly Tory. The Liberals had their political clubs and societies; but most of the students came from families and schools where Conservatism was regarded with the acceptance accorded to the British Constitution or the law of gravitation.

When the aged Gladstone visited Oxford in the early nineties and delivered his Romanes lecture—almost his last public utterance—it was the Oxford scholar, the author of *The Impregnable*

Rock of Holy Scripture, who was received with eager enthusiasm, not the apostle of peace, retrenchment and reform. Ruskin, who believed in none of the three, was supported as long as support was possible. Oxford, like the rest of the country, was not only pre-war, but pre-Boer war. The 'labouring poor' lived in a world of their own; and to take an interest in them was the sign of a mild eccentricity like nonconformity or teetotalism. But here too the leaven was working. Canon Barnett of Whitechapel, with the not very instructed support of the great Jowett behind him, was telling the common-rooms that England was still two nations, and that the only way of avoiding the consequences of such a fatal division was that Oxford men, when they went down, should get to know the poor—live among them in fact. The example set by Toynbee Hall in 1880 was followed by a Settlement in Canning Town due to the enthusiasm of Mansfield College.

Toynbee Hall, however, was not generally regarded as a religious institution. Religion in Oxford counted for much; but for the most part it still meant loyalty to the Church of England as by law established; to be supported, but not to be meddled with, by legislation. Apart from the Liberals and their innovations, two things mainly were to be feared, science and criticism. Evolution had not quite ceased to rouse the hostile ardours that had been kindled at the famous meeting of the British Association in 1851, with its unfortunate duel between Bishop Wilberforce and Thomas Huxley; but of the actual work done by men of science little notice was taken. Degrees were given for science as for mathematics; but few presented themselves for them, or believed in their educational value. Everyone grudged the money that scientific studies were beginning to demand.

Criticism, as it was called, was a different matter. Strauss and Renan, like Ewald and Wellhausen, were regarded with horror as laying the axe at the root of religious belief. Robertson Smith was equally dangerous in Scotland. There was no one in Oxford corresponding to the Cambridge trio of Westcott, Lightfoot, and Hort. Theology was bound up with patristics. Grave divines still shook troubled heads over the memories of *Essays and Reviews;* and even the cautious opinions of Samuel Driver and William Sanday were looked upon, by High Church and Evangelicals alike, with misgiving and dread. Nor was resentment at the conclusions of the critics mere obscurantism. As traditional authorships were questioned, and traditional interpretations discredited, there was a sense of personal loss. Like the orthodox struggling with the Arians in the fourth century, perturbed but earnest Christians cried with a real sinking of the heart: 'They have taken away my Lord.'

The High Church was the leading but not the only brand (if the word may be forgiven) of Anglicanism in the University. The Evangelicals were led by the very popular Canon Chavasse; and Wycliffe Hall, the seminary for Evangelical students for the Anglican ministry, helped to maintain little groups for the study of the Bible in most of the colleges, groups which played their part in the growth of the Student Volunteer Missionary Union and the Student Christian Movement a few years later. J. H. Oldham and Frank Weston were contemporaries in the same college a few years after Peake entered St John's. The High Church party, however, enjoyed the intellectual prestige, and its members feared the Evangelicals less than most of them feared the influence of the philosophers. The strongest of the schools or departments of study in the University was that known as *Literae Humaniores* or more popularly 'Greats'. Its course was based on a close study of the classics, carried on into philosophy, Greek and European. After a hard struggle, led by T. H. Green, what had been the reigning system of T. S. Mill and Herbert Spencer had been vanquished, and Plato and Aristotle were interpreted as leading on to Kant and Hegel.

The orthodoxy of Green himself, one of the most selfless and devoted men whom Oxford had known, was gravely suspected, but the influence which he exercised over the ablest of his students was at one time almost unbounded, and both High Churchmen and Evangelicals regarded it as something of a triumph when a young scholar could go through a course of German philosophy and yet not jettison his faith. Happily for them, neither the students nor their tutors as yet gave a thought to the still (in Oxford) unknown Karl Marx. But Cardinal Newman, whose passing over to Rome had caused a wave of consternation, was now the idol of the High Churchmen. Oxford had loved him as he had always loved Oxford. If, in his later years (he died in 1890) few followed him to Rome, the admiration which he had aroused anchored many the more firmly to the Church which in deep distress he had left forty-five years before. Strange that more did not ask themselves whether the prayer of his pathetic 'Lead kindly Light' had been answered or not.

Such was the Oxford which received the young Arthur Peake into its bosom. And no place, as this brief description makes clear, could have given a greater shock at his first entrance to the young Methodist minister's son. It was the negation of his religious convictions and of the social world in which he had grown up. Why did he choose Oxford instead of Cambridge? Cambridge in those days, if it could not give him all that he might desire, possessed a great deal of what he would seek in vain at Oxford. Cambridge, he might have reflected, had been wont to open her doors to the ideas to which Oxford barred hers. Cambridge was the home of adventures in thought, Oxford of reaction. Cambridge had nurtured Wordsworth; Oxford had rusticated Shelley. It was certainly not the Oxford manner of speech or of bearing that attracted the school-boy. He never learnt them; he never could have done so. He would have to put on a dress coat when he went to dine with a tutor or at the high table; but that was as far as he ever went. Brought up in a Methodist manse, he could not forget that Oxford had been but a step-mother to Methodists from the beginning; and though John Wesley, like John Henry Newman, never lost his affection for the revered walls where he had once worn the gown—he hardly seemed to be aware of the existence of Cambridge—yet to the University, Methodists were no better than the dissenters whom, left to herself, she would never have admitted. Whatever were the reasons that guided his youthful footsteps from Coventry to Oxford, it was a fortunate thing for him that he gained a scholarship at St John's College. He came up with a keen interest in the Old Testament, and St John's had the reputation of providing for those who wished for it as careful a training in Hebrew as in the classical languages. He passed the examination known as Classical Honour Moderations, where Greek and Latin poets and orators were studied side by side with medieval logic; and instead of going on, as most scholars did, to the final classical school, where the student learnt to look at history and philosophy with a mind sharpened by the Greeks, Peake turned to the sister subject of theology, where he gained the First Class that his friends expected.

The award of a further scholarship made it possible for him to remain in Oxford for another three years, in which he gained the

University scholarship known as the Denyer and Johnson, and the Ellerton University Prize; this last was given for an essay on Montanism. Then, in 1890, came a prize fellowship at Merton, which meant residence in Oxford for at least another two years. So, it might seem, were being laid the foundations for a life-long academic career. But while Peake's mind was academic, in one sense of that overworked word, in the other it ended by being the very opposite. To understand the distinction here suggested is vital for an admirer of Peake.

What does the word really signify? Refusing to treat it, with some zealous persons, as a mere term of abuse, we may regard it as firstly standing for the mental processes that with unfailing industry and cold impartiality collect and study, test and correlate, what can be looked on as facts; proving all things, holding fast that which is good. Secondly, the academic mind, to be true to its calling, will pay more attention to the journey than to the end, to the establishment of facts than to what may be considered their value in the world. It has neither the wish nor the intention, to borrow Plato's phrase, to re-enter the cave. It is at home in the University, but a stranger in the universe.

In his first years in Oxford Peake lived in an atmosphere which was academic in both senses of the word, and was breathed in most Oxford lecture rooms. To refer to the subject in which he was most interested: in the study of the Old Testament, as it was being transformed by the Germans, the texts were examined with the minute care long devoted to Aristotle. The results were highly disturbing to most old-fashioned readers in Oxford as well as outside, though they were destined in time to make the Old Testament no longer merely a subject for the study and the examination room, but an arsenal even for the politician and the reformer. The Oxford in which Peake was reading thought but little of this destiny; but Peake was to find himself at the centre of the small but growing band who saw—perhaps at first but dimly—the wider horizon, and determined to make for it.

The same was true of his work on St Paul. His interest in the Old Testament never blinded him to the truth of the maxim *Novum Testamentum in Vetere latet: Vetus in Novo patet*—the New Testament lies hid in the Old, the Old lies open in the New. Those who knew him in Oxford never thought of him simply as an Old Testament scholar. On St Paul, too, the Germans were hard at work in those days. But they would have despised themselves if they had thought of their Paulinism as a subject for a popular pulpit, still more if they had considered it a matter for discussion in a social democratic gathering. When Peake's friends listened to the Pauline papers which he read to them from time to time, they were aware of one who had even then read as widely as most men in Oxford on the subject, but who was beginning to read, and to write, with a new purpose. How that purpose was to be fulfilled might not at the time be very clear; but every book that Peake was to write has made it clearer. One thing stands out. Even in those far-off days, when Moody was paying his second evangelistic visit to the country, Peake had no sympathy with the short and easy methods of expounding St Paul: 'You are sinners; you deserve death; but Christ has died instead of you; believe this and you are free.' Perhaps he found it difficult, as others have done, to distinguish the somewhat slick manner of preaching the Gospel not unknown in his own Methodist denomination, from the duty of reverent waiting on the Word of God laid on every true evangelist. But the Bible was to him no convenient collection of texts or axioms; it was the record of what had been said by holy men of God who had spoken through the centuries as they had been moved by the Spirit.

Then in 1890, seven years after he had come up to St John's, came the call to a tutorship and lectureship at Mansfield. Mansfield had started on its Oxford career only four years before, and there was something romantic about its early beginnings. Nonconformists had now been admitted to the University for fifteen years, but a Congregational College to train men for the dissenting ministries was a different matter. The Principal, Dr A. M. Fairbairn, a distinguished Scottish theologian, fully understood his position. Why, people asked, if Mansfield had to leave the friendly atmosphere of Birmingham, should it come to Oxford and be a lodge, as it were, in a garden of cucumbers? Would it not have been wiser, instead of venturing into a den of lions, to have moved to the milder airs where Westminster and Cheshunt were to find a home and where Ridley Hall would have given the stranger a cordial welcome, far from the subtle corrosion of the Tractarians and their successors?

The founders of Mansfield had their answer. They were aware of a double mission: to train up a body of Free Church ministers, cut loose from the air of the dissenting academy, who would absorb the best that Oxford had to give; and to defend the cause of Nonconformity in the place where it was most in danger of going by default. The new college was generously staffed from the first; but when Peake joined the Staff, an almost ideal combination was formed—Fairbairn, the theologian and philosopher; Vernon Bartlet, the New Testament exegete and Church historian; and Peake, as lecturer in Old Testament subjects and patristics.

The pulpit of the College Chapel was filled in turn by well-known Free Church leaders, like R. F. Horton, Hugh Price Hughes, George Adam Smith. The preacher of the day and the College staff were always present on the Sunday afternoon when the Principal's House welcomed all Nonconformist undergraduates; and a University Theological Society, open to members of all denominations, flourished for some years under the aegis of Mansfield, where, outside the more formal lecture-rooms, young dons and senior undergraduates first became aware of Peake's scholastic powers.

As a religious force Mansfield might have taken as its motto, *Suaviter in modo; fortiter in re*, but the Principal did not always disdain the *fortiter in modo*. Bringing with him a reputation which none could despise or overlook, he preached sermons, like his lectures, as controversial as they were positive, and he took, as it seemed, a genuine delight in exploring the weaknesses of the dominant Anglicanism around him. Bartlet, less controversial in manner, was equally unbending in his adherence to Congregational principles. One of the best and most characteristic things he did was to found, with Dr Sanday, the Society for Historical Theology, flourishing vigorously today. Peake, younger and less formidable than either, with none of the ruggedness of the old Scottish warrior that marked the Principal, and none of the patriarchal amplitude that men smiled at in Bartlet, recalled his hero, Saul of Tarsus, in his bodily presence and his frequent ill-health, and, it must be confessed, the occasional length and obscurity of his sentences. But if his strokes were less cumbrous than theirs, his thrusts were quicker and neater; and at bottom he was as uncompromising as either of them.

Of course he had his eccentricities. You could not go into his comfortable rooms at Merton, people said, without being greeted with 'I was just going to make some tea; have a cup', and his friend A. E. Taylor, who came to the Fellows' Quad at Merton a year after Peake, would say laughingly: 'I am always expecting Peake to ask me to hand him his organic paper-knife'. He and his colleagues had a fine body of students to work on. Sylvester Horne, had he lived, might have been another Hugh Price Hughes; Garvie the uncouth, half Scotch and half Polish, became one of the best known and most revered Free Church Leaders of his time; and a Methodist student once astonished a little company of undergraduates by telling them that, now he had been at Mansfield, he would be the most cultured man in the Methodist ministry. As a matter of fact he was something more.

It was partly ill-health, partly absorption in his work and his preparation for it, and partly a general lack of interest in athletics—a highly unorthodox trait in a young don—which made Peake seem somewhat aloof to his students and to the undergraduates who found in Mansfield a kind of spiritual home. Eager as he was—and his colleagues shared his eagerness—to work out the newer academic ideal, he was hampered, as the younger men felt, by the language of the lecture room which he could not easily throw aside, and by his loyalty to the truth as he conceived it which would sometimes rob his speech and his bearing of the sympathy which was alive beneath both.

The trio was soon broken up. Fairbairn after some years was succeeded by W. B. Selbie (the 'inspired mouse') who as tutor in the first days of the College had been followed by Peake himself. Bartlet lived on for many years, and never moved from Oxford. Peake, after only two years at Mansfield, was summoned to Manchester. Fairbairn's work died with him. No one else could have done it. No successor was needed. Bartlet gained and kept a high place in Oxford, and in the wider world of ecumenical faith and order; and he was often seen at gatherings of the Student Movement and similar if smaller retreats. But as the years went on, his influence contracted, and in the end he slipped quietly away.

Peake, on the other hand, removed to the new world of Manchester. It is not the duty of these pages to follow him. It is enough to say that he found his life's work there. From the very beginning of this fresh chapter in his life he knew, and others knew, that he was in his right place. Others might hint at sacrifice at this removal; he would never have listened to them. For thirty-seven years he was the life and soul of the educational work for the ministry of his own Church. Hartley College and Peake were almost synonymous; and through the College, more effectively than most college tutors, he left his stamp upon the Church. But when Peake came to Manchester, Hartley, if it was his chief, was by no means his only passion. The young University of Manchester was then taking its place as the first of our provincial Universities. It had already attracted a number of distinguished scholars to its Chairs, Conway, Tout, A. E. Taylor, and others; and in 1904 was founded the first interdenominational divinity faculty in a British university. The step was happily aided by the presence in Manchester of a number of divinity colleges. Peake was at once appointed John Rylands Professor of Biblical Exegesis—a post which he held for twenty-five years—while as its first Dean he shaped the school of theology, as Oxford would have called it, into something that Oxford itself might admire, and even envy. He found time—we can hardly call it leisure—to produce a spate of books, books of the very kind whose absence he had deplored in the old Oxford days; and as if he knew of no other commanding interest, he flung himself into all the discussions which paved the way for Methodist union.

All this is fully related in succeeding pages in this book. But those who can see in the redoubtable champion without whom that union might never have been accomplished the young lecturer at Mansfield, may be forgiven if they also see, in the celebrations in 1932, three years after Peake's voice had been stilled, not indeed the fulfilment of a dream, but the completion of a step toward the *major Ecclesia Anglicana*—the phrase is William Sanday's, coined just as Peake's Oxford days were coming to an end—which Oxford with her splendid but chequered history could not but suggest, but to which she herself had never consented.

Thus the brief period spent at Oxford, though almost inarticulate compared with the immense production of the years that followed, needs the illumination of Manchester. But the thirty-seven years at Manchester, one may say with confidence, would have been impossible without it; and this, we may surmise, for three reasons: because of what was given to him by the decade (it was hardly as much as that); because of what was withheld by it; and because of what, unconsciously it may be, it induced into his life.

As for the first of the three, Peake took from Oxford to Manchester a rich store of knowledge, the technique of its advancement and its varied development, and that wide and admiring acquaintance with all that the world will not willingly allow to die which we commonly call culture. There is no need here to enlarge upon an endowment so completely justified. For the second, other things Oxford had not given, had not indeed possessed them to give—for example, the generous recognition of those who prayed in another fashion and who had ceased to suspect impiety in 'field preaching', the readiness to allow venerable but growingly outworn traditions to be questioned, and the sympathy with those who had and could have but the *foi du charbonnier* as Peake's friend A. E. Taylor loved to call it. But there is a sense in which to withhold is itself to give. Peake was not the only man, even in his own days, who, looking in vain at Oxford for what Oxford above all others might have given, determined the more firmly to seek it and to labour for it elsewhere, and who left Oxford in fact a stouter Free Church champion than when he entered it. All the principles in whose presence the boy had been brought up called for their defence by the student and as a result he spent the remainder of his life in serving every one of them.

The third matter is less obvious. The best of Peake's work, long and varied as it is, contains scarcely anything that could be called a *magnum opus*, though his admirers, not without reason, hoped that at least one was on its way. There are the three Commentaries on Jeremiah, Job, and Hebrews; there are numbers of general and semi-popular works on the Bible and its significance, *Faded Myths* among them; there are the monographs on Elijah, on the 'Servant', on Paul, and the rest, many of them published as *Bulletins* of the Rylands Library; there are one or two volumes of essays that he has edited; and there is the *Commentary* by which probably he is and will be best known. None of these has the weight of Robertson Smith's *Religion of the Semites*, Buchanan Gray's *Sacrifice in the Old Testament*, or the great German treatises. Even the commentaries are chiefly valuable as collections of all that is best in what had been previously said about the three books, and the great one-volume *Commentary* contains only eleven articles (though these are among the most important) from his pen.

This however was characteristic of him. I do not know whether he ever quoted to himself Falstaff's words, 'I am not only witty myself; I am the cause of wit in other men', but his great object was the dissemination of all knowledge by those who were best fitted to spread it; and disseminators, as Francis Bacon saw, work best in a team. This is the true ideal of the University: the pursuit of the *omne scibile* by *omnes qui scibunt*, learning, working and teaching together. Whether Peake learnt this from Oxford, I never heard him say. He certainly learnt it at Oxford and he carried it with him from Oxford to Manchester. And surely we may say that the seventh heaven of Paradise, the heaven of the great doctors of theological learning, is still entered by those who decided not to live but know, and whose faces shine with a fresh light of joy whenever opportunity is given them to share with others what He whose Name is Truth has shared with them.

W. F. LOFTHOUSE

MANCHESTER UNIVERSITY

DURING the quarter of a century (1880–1904) of the life of the old federal Victoria University, there were two abortive attempts to establish a Faculty of Theology. Both originated in Owens College, Manchester, and both foundered on the hostility or indifference of the other constituent Colleges in Leeds and Liverpool to the idea of such a Faculty. This development had therefore to wait until the three Colleges became separate Universities. Once that had been done there was rapid progress. The new Charter of the Victoria University of Manchester was issued on 15th July 1903, and by December of that year the University Court had sanctioned the establishment of a Faculty of Theology. At the same time Mrs Rylands the Foundress of the Rylands Library, endowed a Chair of Biblical Criticism and Exegesis in the University. The first occupant of the new Chair and the first Dean of the new Faculty was A. S. Peake. He held the Deanship during the critical years (1904–8) when the Faculty was establishing itself as an integral part of the University, with its own vital contribution to make to the life and work of the whole academic society. He held the Professorship till his lamented death in 1929; and so for twenty-five years represented the Faculty and its interests on the Senate of the University. As one who has had in more recent times considerable experience of both tasks, I welcome the opportunity of paying tribute to the sterling work done by Peake for the Faculty and the University in those formative years.

We may look first at his work as Rylands Professor of Biblical Criticism and Exegesis. Here he set a standard which neither of his successors has attempted to emulate; and it seems likely enough that no future holder of the Chair will be more adventurous than they. For he understood Biblical Criticism and Exegesis quite simply as covering everything from Genesis to Revelation, and proved his competence in this very wide field both by the spoken word and by published work. He also made it plain that in his branch of study there was one aim only, the discovery of the truth, and one method only, the most careful sifting and weighing of all the relevant evidence. By the quality of his work he showed that theological scholarship was intellectually respectable, that theology was not a soft option, and that as a scholarly discipline and a field for research it made as rigorous demands and offered as good opportunities for original and creative work as any other branch of scholarship. He showed this not only in his own lectures, articles, and books, but also in the high standards which, under his leadership, the newly constituted Faculty set for its students. From the outset it was made plain to them that nothing less than the best would be offered to them and expected from them. So the Faculty made its way in the life of the University, not by making extravagant claims and promises, but by going about its business in an honest, diligent, and workmanlike manner. And there was none more capable than Peake of showing just what had to be done, and how to do it.

As first Dean of the Faculty he had a major share in working out the principles that have governed the relations between the University and the Theological Colleges. His position in Hartley College and his Professorship in the University gave him ample opportunity to build the necessary bridges; and there can be no finer testimony to the quality of his building than the simple fact that the history of the Faculty is the history of fifty years of friendly and wholehearted co-operation between the University and the Colleges. It was no accident, as it is no secret, that when, at a much later time, the University was faced with the task of creating a School of Education, in which University and Training Colleges should work together, the conviction that the thing could be done and the first indications of how it might be done, came from a consideration of what had already been achieved in the field of Theology.

The conditions under which Universities and Theological Colleges do their work have changed greatly since 1904 and in the last two or three decades the changes have been most marked and rapid. In those early days it was not just that Didsbury College and Lancashire Independent College had a longer history than Owens College. It was that the resources of Colleges and University were fairly comparable, having regard to their several tasks. The stronger Colleges could each afford to carry a complete Faculty of its own. I have no first-hand knowledge of the early days in Manchester, but I knew Westminster College, Cambridge, when it was staffed by Skinner, Oman, Anderson Scott, and Carnegie

Simpson, and Mansfield College, Oxford, with Selbie, Buchanan Gray, Dodd, and Vernon Bartlet; and I know that there are names no less eminent for the Colleges in Manchester. The University, on the other hand, had large responsibilities and limited financial resources. It was inevitable that it should rely a great deal on the Colleges for help in teaching. That help was readily given to the great benefit of both University and Colleges. Now times have changed; and it is only the Colleges that are directly supported by strong Churches that can afford to carry a full teaching staff. At the same time the amount of financial backing for Universities has gone up by leaps and bounds through the Treasury grants administered by the University Grants Committee. One result of this is that the University is able to do more than ever before for its Theological Faculty. It can provide more teaching staff, more accommodation, better library facilities, more scholarships for post-graduate study. All these things can be helpful to Colleges living in the modern world where income has the greatest difficulty in keeping up with 'overheads', and it speaks well for the relations established in Peake's day that mutual friendliness and helpfulness are as much a reality today as ever they have been.

Only once did I meet the man himself; it was at a meeting of the Society for Old Testament Study. I had arrived early, a young and very new member. I made my way to the Common Room which we were to use, and found one other occupant, an elderly, rather tired-looking man resting on a sofa. He rose and introduced himself as Peake. Up till then I knew of him as a man who had the temerity to hold a different view from Skinner's on the identification of the Servant of Yahweh in Deutero-Isaiah. We talked for a while. Nothing of any great moment was said; but the gracious friendliness of the man made a lasting impression on me. It was only a fleeting glimpse, but it is still vivid; and looking back I think I understand better how the foundations laid fifty years ago have proved so solid and enduring. Something of Peake's own strength, wisdom, and kindness must have been built into them.

T. W. MANSON

AUTHOR AND EDITOR

My acquaintance with Dr Peake began when I was a schoolboy. I had sat for a scholarship at Oxford and had had no word of the result, and so in the stress of anxiety I wrote to Dr Peake, whom I did not know, and asked him for his advice. I had got his name and his photograph from the *Christian Endeavour Year Book*, price twopence! He was very much interested and straightway helped me to get into touch with various people, and, as the scholarship came along shortly after, I was able to go to Oxford.

From that time onward he always treated me as one of the family, and I stayed with him a good deal in his various houses. We used on those occasions to sit up till three in the morning discussing every sort of problem under the sun, and I learnt a great deal about the world and about books and about Dr Peake himself. They were wonderful times of fellowship.

One day he sent me the first book that I had ever been given to review. It was J. N. Figgis's *The Political Theory of St Augustine*. That was in 1921, and from then onward I had from him a succession of books to review for the *Holborn Review*, and I learnt the art of reading quickly and of summarizing. It so happened that my special field, so to speak, was one with which he himself, for a wonder, was totally unacquainted, and that was medieval philosophy and theology. Consequently everything that touched upon that subject was sent to me, and in the course of time I reviewed the whole of the *Cambridge Medieval History*, all the works of Coulton, and a large number of others. It was a wonderful stroke of luck to have hit on a subject which Peake confessed he did not know and in which he was not very much interested.

As an editor he was quite ruthless, at any rate to his friends. He might know nothing about the subject, but he knew how it ought to be handled. He many a time sent a review back to me to be 'corrected', as he called it, and on two occasions he wrote this comment at the bottom of a review in which I had put in a certain number of Latin tags: 'Are these really necessary or are you just showing off?' That was a pretty bitter remark to make, because his second alternative was nearer the truth! He did teach me to be simple, clear, direct, and to cut out all frills.

That was his own way of writing, and he carried it into his criticism of the work that people sent in for the *Holborn Review*. Consequently he made the 'Holborn' one of the very best quarterlies in the country. Quite often more than half of it would be taken up by reviews, and the publishers were very pleased to send in even expensive books. I have known Anglican scholars and others with no connexion with the Methodist Church who regularly subscribed to the 'Holborn' for the sake of Peake's reviews. In biblical studies and theology he seemed to have read everything, and to know everything, and a word of commendation from him was a very good advertisement.

In my early days of reviewing he insisted on my buying a book by Robert Lynd in which there was an article on the art of reviewing. Peake, following Lynd, had no use for the type of review that assumes that if only the reviewer had been given the job of writing the book how much better it would have been. He insisted that the first task of the reviewer was to tell the reader what the book was about, whether he himself agreed with it or not. (How very few reviewers follow that simple rule, even at times the highbrows in the *Times Literary Supplement!*) Then the reviewer had to say a word of commendation if it could be said sincerely, and then plunge into his criticism, which need not, of course, be hostile. Peake understood criticism in its original sense of assessing a situation rather than attacking it. Consequently his own reviews were in themselves original short treatises on the subject of the books. While commending the work of other people he would give in brief outline an account of the situation with which the book itself dealt, and show how the author had something new to offer, if indeed it was that kind of book. On looking over some past numbers of the 'Holborn' I have been very much struck by the way in which Peake's reviews were an education in the subject with which they dealt. Perhaps one reason for this was that he himself was very cautious of expressing points of view; sometimes his lectures were a little irritating on that account. He told you what everybody else had said on a subject and never told you what he himself believed. This modesty, or, some would say, timidity, nevertheless made him a very fair and discerning critic, and I feel quite sure that many of the authors must have been grateful to him.

When the *Commentary* came along most other things were cleared out of the way to make room for it. I am glad to think that I had a small share in it, and found him one of his commentators, but I did often wonder whether the sheer donkey-work put into that book was really altogether worth it. I think perhaps it was, with the exception of the index. He spent months over the index and even then it was not so helpful as he intended it to be. For instance, if you look up the work 'king' in the index there are ninety-two numbers attached, but which is the one that you desire is by no means easy to discover unless you work through the whole lot! Peake, however, was certain that this was the way to do things, and the index is a marvel of sheer routine hard work. It covers sixty-eight pages of three columns each, small print. I remember visiting him once when he was 'on holiday' at Barnard Castle, and on a lovely afternoon found him and his indefatigable secretary, Miss Cann, in a shelter at the bottom of the garden, wrestling with the index! It was like St Bernard pacing the shores of Lake Geneva with his cowl over his head, and I said so, but Peake didn't mind. He felt that the index was a service to mankind.

It was not only the index, however, that was characteristic of his work. If you look through the book anywhere you will come across interpolations in square brackets which he himself put in. He went over every single word of every commentator, and where he thought some remark was needed he inserted it. He also persuaded his writers to drop the prefix 'St' or 'S.' on the ground that 'the use of reverential epithets tends to interpose a veil between the modern reader and faces already too dim'. He had great difficulties with many of his writers because they would not send up material in time, and although he was very patient, at the same time he often had occasion to deal firmly and indeed severely with some of them. He used to say that it was much easier to write a book by yourself than to get a dozen people to write it for you.

His other books are all marked by the same meticulous scholarship and cautious judgement. In his more popular book, however, *Christianity: Its Nature and Truth*, he was not so much dealing with a subject as expressing a witness, and so he could let himself go. Probably that is the book by which he is generally best known to people outside the world of theology. He twice gave the Hartley Lecture, and on the first occasion in 1904 he dealt with the problem of suffering in the Old Testament, a subject with which he was always very much concerned. He never, however, got down to his projected book on Isaiah in the International Critical Commentary series. I used to remind him of this again and again, but I think his attitude was that his main job was that of a middleman, not so much doing original work himself as presenting the results of it to the ordinary ranks of the ministry and the laity. He was thus a great interpreter of other men's work. A book, for instance, called *Faded Myths*, although very slight, was a great help to people who were wanting to know a little more about the present view of the Old Testament.

The Old Testament had his first love, and the little book in the Century Bible Handbooks on the religion of Israel was quite a small classic in its way. Of his commentaries the Century Bible *Job* is outstanding, and so too is his *Hebrews* in the New Testament series, for it had this Old Testament reference of which he was so good an expositor. His *Jeremiah* in two volumes dealt with a personality that was very near to his heart, and when he went to Palestine on a visit it was to Anathoth that his first interest was directed. Even his interest in Paul was very largely due to the Hebraic roots of what he called 'Paulinism'. In his excellent introduction to the symposium *The People and the Book* he commends the writers for their recognition that the Old Testament is the 'indispensable approach to the right interpretation of the New Testament'. He greatly enjoyed his editorship of this book, and it was a great grief to him that his friend George Buchanan Gray died before it could be published. He got his fourteen collaborators to agree to dedicate the volume to Gray's memory.

One of the earliest symposia was the collection of Inaugural Lectures delivered by the members of the Faculty of Theology at Manchester during its first session 1904–5. He himself contributed a lecture on the 'Present Movement of Biblical Science' (the use of the word 'science' is significant in this context), and as Dean of the Faculty he introduced the lecturers in a very interesting preface. He pointed out that each lecturer had been free to go his own way, but that 'though the standard of popular treatment fluctuates, the lectures should be judged as intended for those who, while interested in theology, are not theologians. The University sinks below the level of its privilege and duty unless it hears the call to share the gains of scholarship with those whose life runs in other grooves.' He goes on from that to quote a remark of

Harnack: 'The theologians of every country only half discharge their duties if they think it enough to treat of the Gospel in the recondite language of learning, and bury it in scholarly folios.' This judgement seems to have had a great influence upon him, for from this time onward he felt that he had a special vocation to popularize the historical study of the Bible.

For this reason he welcomed every opportunity to speak and to write on his favourite theme. For the Brotherhood Movement he gave an address on Brotherhood in the Old Testament, and he had a cheap edition published of his book, *Christianity: Its Nature and Truth*. He also joined with R. G. Parsons, afterwards Bishop of Middleton, in editing a five-volume work, *The Outline of Christianity*, which was projected by a popular publishing house. He was a convinced Protestant and Free Churchman, and perhaps the best single thing he ever did was his address to the Bridlington meeting of the Free Church Council. It was notable for his critical handling of the Roman Catholic use of the texts in Matthew on which they base the claim of the supremacy of Peter. He had many Roman Catholic friends, and indeed he got on well with most people, but he had a strong bias in favour of historical truth.

I only once heard him lecture, and that was when he came up to Oxford in 1910 to lecture on Methodism in a series afterwards published under the title of *Evangelical Christianity*. It was an interesting occasion in many ways. Peake belonged to the Primitive Methodist Church, in those days considered by the Wesleyans as something of a 'sport' on the Wesleyan tree, and consequently unable properly to represent 'Methodism' as such. There were some therefore who felt that he was not the best choice for this subject, but when the lecture came off there was no doubt that the Committee had chosen the right man. It was an astonishing lecture, delivered entirely without notes, scholarly and amusing and holding the interest of the audience all the while. It was delivered in Mansfield College, where he himself had begun his career as a lecturer and which was very congenial ground. He loved Mansfield, which in those days was a notable centre of evangelical religion as well as sound scholarship. It was by his wish and with his help that I myself joined the college later as a student under Dr Selbie.

A. VICTOR MURRAY

ECUMENICAL CHURCHMAN

ARTHUR SAMUEL PEAKE was a man of profound ecumenical sympathies, which deepened with the passing of the years. In a letter written in his undergraduate days there is early evidence of this. 'I can never be satisfied till we have gained an organic unity. This unity will never be gained till we consent to sink differences of belief, and make Christ the foundation on which we build. . . . For myself I don't care to be called either Methodist, or Church of England, or Protestant, or any name except Christian.' The essence of that youthful enthusiasm never forsook him. It was on this ground that he gave abundance of time and effort to the cause of reunion in all the after years.

I

To the early impulses toward understanding and co-operation between the Methodist Churches Peake soon gave allegiance. In particular, he attended the meetings of the Methodist Assembly in 1909, which was formed to increase fellowship and stimulate action, although no reference was made to organic union. Peake contributed to the occasion, and afterwards wrote:

The movement thus happily initiated must be carried forward. . . . No good can come of any attempts to force an organic union; rather we should seek all opportunities of fellowship and co-operation that we may be prepared for an easy and natural union when the time is ripe.

In 1913 the Wesleyan Conference appointed a committee to explore the possibilities of uniting the various branches of the Methodist Church but the War prevented its implementation. In 1918, however, at the three Conferences, resolutions were passed appointing a committee to take up the work and submit proposals to the Conference of the following year. The two smaller Churches passed the resolution unanimously, and at the Wesleyan Conference only two opposing votes were registered. Shortly afterwards in Manchester at an informal lunch of representative Methodists of all branches, Peake spoke on behalf of the Primitive Methodist Church. This may be regarded as his public entry into the movement.

During the first stage Peake's contribution lay in exposition of his own convictions on the whole subject, and therein he gave important leadership. He was certain that union, both in spirit and organization, was the ideal of Christ for His Church. The great similarities between the Methodist Churches far outweighed any differences. Moreover the whole Church suffered in the eyes of men because of its divisions, and a united Church would provide a new instrument for evangelization as it confronted the forces of evil. Further, the concept of reunion was becoming more widespread, and he was convinced that a Methodist Church united in one organization would be an important factor in the promotion of a still wider union.

Certain principles naturally governed Peake's work for this cause. He constantly urged the necessity of being willing to surrender prejudice to principle, not least when self-interest tended to assert itself or when an impasse had been reached. Further, when any suggestion that negotiation should be brought to an end he urged that the will of the people must be ascertained through their representative courts before such suspension could be morally justified.

Amidst the impatience that was inevitable because progress was often slow, Peake would indicate the solemn and serious responsibility of deciding to abandon the scheme, and pleaded that if in the end a refusal had to come it should not be those of his own Church who incurred such grave decision. His place and attitude in these negotiations bring to mind the entreaties of Baxter at the Savoy Conference in 1661, as he stood between the two parties, the one side having to be sustained in their endeavours and those of the other side to be persuaded into conviction. Throughout the negotiations Peake appealed above all for elasticity both in doctrine and organization.

The first flush of widespread enthusiasm for union was inevitably followed by intensive criticism. Between the years 1920 and 1925 Peake gave time and energy to a leadership that again and again was to prove decisive. By patient explanation he pointed out that, although there might be difference in the distribution of emphasis, yet the lines of division, whether theological or ecclesiastical, by no means coincided with the lines of denominational cleavage. Above all he deprecated 'the manufacture of differences which had no substantial existence' and urged that the particular type of evangelism which belonged to his own denomination was no longer the monopoly of Primitive Methodism, and had for a long time ceased to be specially characteristic of that group.

Nowhere more than in the framing of the doctrinal standards of the united Church did Peake show greater sagacity. He confessed that he would have preferred a doctrinal statement of a more general kind and the omission of any reference to Wesley's *Notes* and *Sermons* from such statement,[1] but he recognized that behind this reference there lay a sense of the value of continuity and also a constant reminder of the heritage of the Evangelical Revival. Moreover in the phrase 'generally contained' he felt there was an adequate safeguard against anything beyond a general acceptance of this evangelical position. He urged the significance of the natural loyalty felt by the Wesleyans for their great founder, and he reminded those of his own denomination that their own declared articles of faith were in part obsolete. His discussions of this doctrinal issue became decisive for many, and were described at the time as 'historic'.

Another instance of Peake's sagacity is seen in his exposition of the nature and office of the ministry. His interpretation went far to dissolve the fear of sacerdotalism which undoubtedly existed in the smaller denominations, and the fear of a lowering of ministerial position which existed equally in the larger group. Much of this discussion centred in the proposal that the Pastoral Session should continue as part of the new order. Although hesitant at first—for in Primitive Methodism there was no organization composed exclusively of ministers—Peake became convinced of its value and accepted it as part of the scheme. His commitment went far to turn the scale in favour of its inclusion.

Allied to this was Peake's exposition of the ministerial office. There was some body of opinion in the larger Church which tended to suggest that this group held a higher conception of its ministry than was the case in the smaller groups. This Peake strongly repudiated as an entirely false view. He wrote:

So far as the ministry is concerned there is a real difference in practice and no doubt a certain difference in emphasis. But the difference can

---

[1] The following indicates some ground of Peake's hesitancy on this point. 'It is obvious that Wesley's exegesis of the New Testament, which was confessedly derived from Bengel, has frequently to be rejected. His whole exposition of the Book of the Revelation, also derived from Bengel, is radically unsound.' Art. 'Methodist Union: The Doctrinal Statement' (*Primitive Methodist Leader*, 19th February 1920). He recognized that Wesley's interest was 'not a speculative but a practical interest'.

hardly be described as essential. . . . Some ministers are in danger of emphasizing the ministerial function and prerogative more than is morally good for them, and are exposed to the temptation of unduly depreciating the laity. . . . On the other hand it is possible that where lay-co-operation is more extensive, this may react on the estimation of the ministers. But that is hardly my experience. When I heard it explained in the early days of the Union Committee that the Wesleyans did not regard their ministers as 'the paid agents of the Church' I asked myself in amazement what Methodist people entertained so grovelling a view of the ministry. It was, with more than half-a-century's experience of Primitive Methodism, being myself a minister's son, entirely unfamiliar to me. The description of it as the highest calling open to a man, the most sacred vocation, one not to be taken save on the warrant of a Divine call authenticated by the call of the Church—all this was familiar to me. . . . I repudiate with hot indignation, as one whose life is dedicated to the training of the ministry, the opinion that we value it so lightly. . . . Be it ours to have a high doctrine of the ministry just because we have a high doctrine of the Church, to regard the ministry not as possessed of any priesthood which it does not share with the laity, but to recognize that that priesthood finds its fittest organ and most intense expression in the activities of those who are wholly dedicated to its service. If anyone thinks of a grace different in quality, which is not the possession of the whole priestly body, I repudiate this as wholly at variance with the New Testament teaching on the Church. And in this I rejoice to believe that the vast body of Wesleyan opinion is with me.[1]

Peake's strong and patient interpretation did more than any other factor to assuage the deep tide of feeling on both sides. It should be remembered that at this crucial stage in the movement some eight hundred Wesleyan ministers signed a manifesto against union. To this Peake replied in a lengthy article which was printed in all the Methodist Papers, and his criticism made a profound impression that went far to dissolve the bitterness that had been engendered.[2] These references are not made in any sense in order

[1] *P.M.L.*, Art. 'Methodist Union Opposition', 8th June 1922.
[2] The Manifesto referred to 'the valuable historic individuality' of the Wesleyan Church and continued: 'We believe that the obliteration of the Wesleyan type would inflict a real loss upon the Universal Church. . . . We hold that the viewpoint of Wesleyan Methodism is essentially different from that of the other Methodist Churches in regard to doctrinal standards, the Sacraments, forms of worship, the ministry, party politics and other matters of first importance. The proposed scheme of union involves a large accession of those whose sentiment and training will inevitably lead farther and farther away from the Wesleyan tradition and usages.'

to revive unhappy battles of long ago, but simply to indicate how crucial was Peake's influence in dissolving the bitterness that arose because of these things, and which might well have caused the collapse of the whole union movement.

During this most critical period Peake's influence was felt in yet another matter, namely the question of the Sacrament of the Lord's Supper. He preferred that the service should be conducted by a minister, and that on several grounds: it conformed to the normal practice of Christendom, the minister stood in close pastoral relation to the congregation, and he was likely to conduct the service in a smoother manner than a layman less accustomed to the practice. Nevertheless he believed that there was no New Testament evidence that declared that a layman could *not* perform the office in the absence of a minister. He knew also that within the Methodist structure there were many small country churches that could only be visited by a circuit minister on rare occasions, and therefore he felt that for such congregations this meant a denial of reasonably frequent participation in the Sacrament. He therefore advocated that laymen, duly appointed for the work, should be set aside and should act as representatives of the Church. They could be local preachers, though not necessarily so, for he believed that this duty was closely allied to the pastoral ministry of the class-leader. Such advocacy arose out of Peake's conviction that it is for the living Church to create its own organization and to modify it or expand it as new conditions arise and new needs have to be met.

As the background of this concern for matters theological and ecclesiastical during this crucial period, Peake's great contribution was the upholding of patience and goodwill within his own Church at a time when the negotiations were not seldom prolonged and even wearisome. He wrote significantly: 'If the negotiations are ultimately wrecked may the responsibility not lie at the door and be a burden on the conscience of the Primitive Methodist Church! If the great refusal has to be made let it not be said that it was we who have made it.'[1]

In 1925 the scheme was referred to all three Conferences for sanction, with the requirement of a seventy-five per cent majority to be secured. The Conference of the Primitive Methodist and the United Methodist Churches voted strongly in favour, the vote of

[1] *P.M.L.*, 20th November 1924.

the former, when Peake moved the resolution, being 93 per cent. In the Wesleyan Conference, however, the vote fell short of the required majority. The scheme was therefore referred to the Drafting Committee to report to the Conference of the following year. Again it was Peake who by his spirit of conciliation proved invaluable at this crisis. Two amendments were adopted by the committee: the first concerned doctrine and emphasized the claim of Methodism to belong to the Church Catholic; the second concerned the administration of the Lord's Supper and was designed to secure more elasticity and, in particular, more frequent observance. Previously it had been decided that each of the three Churches should, for the time being, continue its own practice; it was now decided to adopt the suggestion which Peake had recommended, namely that if no minister could be present, the Quarterly Meeting was empowered to elect a suitable layman to administer.

At the Conference of his own Church Peake declared that he himself had had the privilege of drafting these amendments for the Committee, and stated that the first amendment brought the new Methodist Church into line with the great affirmations of the Church Catholic, and that behind the second there lay the vital principle of the priesthood of all believers and its adoption would strengthen the place of the Sacrament in the life of the Church.

At the same Conference Peake spoke to the main resolution about Union, reminding the assembly that a very critical moment in the history of the negotiations had now been reached. He declared that it would be a tragic decision if Primitive Methodism reversed its previous policy of support. The voting resulted in 167 for and 26 against the scheme. Such was the judgement after eight years of endeavour. Unfortunately once again the Wesleyan Conference failed to secure the required majority.

In the Conference of the following year, 1927, Peake was again entrusted with the moving of the resolution, and once more, with typical caution, he declared that any false step would be dangerous, and that an impatient attitude could not be justified. This time the voting issued in 190 for and 22 against. Yet again the Wesleyan Conference failed to obtain a sufficient majority.

At the Conference of 1928 the subject was presented for the tenth time, and again it was to Peake that the piloting of the debate was committed. He appealed for the spirit of patient understanding and reminded the assembly that they were legislating for future generations; it was nothing less than the struggle of the Methodist Church for future efficiency. The voting resulted in a majority of 89 per cent—after ten years of debate!

There is no question that the persistent triumph throughout these years was due largely, if not entirely, to the strong, quiet and persuasive insistence of Peake, whose advocacy had its influence in the other Methodist communions.

The same year the Wesleyan Conference procured the requisite majority, and early in 1929, Peake was appointed as one of the number to give evidence before the Parliamentary Committee in connexion with a Methodist Union Enabling Bill.

In August of that year Peake died. The land he had so wished to enter he saw—but entered not. The consummation so devoutly wished he never experienced.

Two contemporary testimonies can form a fitting estimate of the immense importance of Peake's work for this cause. Dr Wilbert F. Howard wrote:

Writing as a Wesleyan Methodist I must testify to the great influence which Dr Peake's handling of the Union question had upon many in my own Church. There were not a few on our side who feared that the two smaller Churches in their traditional dislike of clericalism would hold in too light esteem elements in our usage which our own experience has shown us to be of utmost value in the development of a strong and healthy churchmanship. Others of our number hesitated to press for a high doctrine of the Church lest they might seem to be advocating sacerdotalism—a heresy as repugnant to Wesleyans as to Primitive Methodists. It was here that Dr Peake's lofty conception of the Christian Society raised us up above the comparatively petty differences of denominational custom and usage. As he expounded the New Testament doctrine of the Church he drew together men of diverse temperaments and traditions. If reunited Methodism holds up to the world in its teaching about the Body of Christ the noble doctrine which Paul set forth in the Epistle to the Ephesians, we shall owe this more to Dr Peake than to any other man.[1]

The following came from the pen of Dr Scott Lidgett:

The great qualities of Dr Peake's character did as much as his eminent intellectual gifts and scholarship to make his great achievement possible. To unreserved consecration, high courage and loyalty to truth, he added

[1] *Holborn Review* (1930), p. 32.

a sincerity of spirit, sympathetic insight and untiring patience. The weight of his convictions was always accompanied by sweet reasonableness of temper and by the balanced judgements of wisdom. Hence the results at which he arrived were expounded with lucidity, upheld with courtesy and gentleness, and brought to acceptance by careful and conciliating presentation. In maintaining his own he put himself at the other man's point of view.

All these qualities were displayed in Dr Peake's great contribution to the cause and triumph of Methodist Union. During its long drawn-out proceedings the United Committee had to encounter at times serious dangers and possible crises. It surmounted them all, and did so, not by mere bargaining or artificial arrangements, but because 'the unity of the spirit in the bond of peace' was steadfastly preserved. And no man did more to secure, by God's blessing, this great result than Dr Peake. Here his clear vision of the end, his tenacity in pursuing it, and his patience in overcoming obstacles, were conspicuous and uniformly successful.[1]

II

We have already observed that Peake's labours for Methodist Union were set in the context of a concern for the reunion of Christendom. It was for this reason that he gave his energies to bringing nearer the fulfilment of that ideal. In this matter of wider union he was convinced that the Church of England was of pivotal importance, and that a Union between the Anglican and the Free Churches was probably the most immediate step, once Methodist Union was achieved. He recognized, however, that the Anglican Church had affinities with the Lutheran, the Reformed, and the Evangelical Churches on the one hand, and with the Eastern and Latin Churches on the other. This situation at once demanded extreme caution on the part of the Church of England lest the relations with the Eastern and Latin Churches should be endangered. Peake believed also that the Free Churches should be equally cautious lest relations with non-episcopalian Churches elsewhere should become imperilled. He had also a clear conviction as to the problem of any attempt in the direction of union with Rome, believing that, in the Roman view, the only possibility was submission to the Roman Church as the one true Church; the real issue lay beyond the realms of discussion. As to the Eastern Churches, Peake also felt that reunion was at best a remote possibility, though there was some hopefulness in the fact that

[1] Ibid. pp. 38-9.

discussion of such matters was not rejected, and also that the Eastern Churches were not bound by any dogma of papal infallibility. For the Anglican Church to look in the direction of Rome was to look for the impossible; to look in the direction of the Eastern Churches was at most a hope that implied a very far prospect; on the other hand, to look toward the Free Churches was to envisage a real possibility of accommodation.

In his thought upon reunion at home, Peake was naturally concerned with the nature of the Church, the doctrine of the Ministry involving the problems of Episcopacy, Ordination, and the Sacraments, and in addition the relation of Church and State. It was for this reason that he regarded the Federal Council of the Evangelical Free Churches as supremely important for the examination of these problems, and he regularly attended the meetings of the Council. In 1927 as President of the National Free Church Council he carefully expounded his convictions in an address which may be rightly described as of historic significance. As the text of this address is printed in this present volume[1] it is not necessary here even to summarize his position in these matters.

We may note, however, two instances of the depth of his convictions. His response to the *Appeal to all Christian People* issued from Lambeth in 1920 was wholehearted. He wrote:

Its importance is universally recognized alike for its temper and the actual proposals it makes. The proposals themselves may be unacceptable: but the surprising advance in spirit ought to receive the warmest and fullest welcome, the most cordial and ungrudging recognition. There ought to be no reserve in recognizing the entire sincerity of the approach to the Free Churches and the desire to heal the breaches in the visible unity of the Church. There is one point to which I desire to call special attention, and that is the deep conviction of Divine Guidance which filled the assembly, the consciousness of the presence and influence of the Holy Spirit.[2]

As Peake presented the implications of this historic declaration to the Conference of his own Church in 1921, we see him once again stepping forth as a leader of thought and action.

The first and last feeling that should be in our hearts should be one of unreserved recognition of the spirit and temper of the Lambeth

---

[1] Pp. 143–59.   [2] *Holborn Review* (1920), p. 392.

Appeal. It is a Christian document from beginning to end . . . a new note is struck. . . . In this appeal there is the real presence of Christ who Himself is calling us along this path. . . . Our immediate duty is not to think about ultimate terms of reunion, but with the utmost warmth of spirit to reciprocate the temper that lies behind this Appeal. . . . From this great movement a new era is beginning for all.[1]

The resolution of commendation of the Appeal was carried unanimously.

In the following September the Federal Council appointed a committee of representatives to meet those of the Anglican Church, and from it a sub-committee of four Bishops, two Anglican theologians, and six Free Churchmen, under the chairmanship of the Archbishop of York, was appointed to continue discussion. Of this sub-committee Peake was a member. He declared his attitude with clearness:

Our first duty to those who are separated from us is not to refute but to understand them. Of all qualities in this connexion that of sympathetic imagination is most to be prized, the quality which enables us to slip out of our theological and ecclesiastical prepossessions and to survey the situation from the standpoint and with the eyes of those from whom we dissent. Nor must we ever forget that the Church is no human institution merely, but a Divine creation. It is the Body of Christ, the sensitive and responsive organ through which He functions on earth. It is the Bride of Christ, chosen by Him before the foundation of the world, to be His own, bought with a price, redeemed at the cost of His blood, cleansed by His Spirit, destined at the last to be presented to Him in her radiant glory and free from spot or wrinkle or any such thing. It is the Temple of the Holy Ghost, not meant to be rent by schism or defaced by unseemly rivalries. We are not abandoned to our dimness of insight, defective wisdom or perversity of will. And where we can see no outlet, God may find the way.[2]

In 1926, following the discussions of the intervening years, the Conference of the Primitive Methodist Church made an official reply to the Lambeth Appeal, and it was to Peake that the drafting of the letter was entrusted. It forms one further illustration of his far-reaching sagacity.[3]

[1] *P.M.L.*, 20th June 1921.
[2] From an address, 'The Reunion of Christendom', given to the Unity Meeting of the Wesleyan Conference at Sheffield in July 1922 (*P.M.L.*, 3rd August 1922). The final report of this Joint Committee under the title 'Church Unity' may be found in *Documents on Christian Unity*, ed. G. K. A. Bell (1924).
[3] *Documents on Christian Unity*, ed. G. K. A. Bell (Second Series), p. 108.

The second instance is seen in Peake's association with the Conference of Faith and Order held at Lausanne in 1927, of which he was a member. He regarded this Conference as 'the most important event in the religious world for many a long day'. In commending its importance he declared:

The great thing at present is to create the right atmosphere and acquire a sympathetic insight into points of view other than our own. ... We must all be prepared to examine our first principles afresh and see whether they are wholly matters of principle, or whether they may not be rooted in custom, tradition or even prejudice. We rightly expect that others should do this, we cannot evade the challenge to do it ourselves. The trouble with all reunion movements is that there is on both sides a solid body of opinion obstinately entrenched in the conviction that its own position is impregnable, and viewing any attempt to criticize its own presuppositions and conclusions or strive impartially to appreciate the truth held by the other party as selling the pass. ... This may be a far-off Divine event, but we should cherish it as an ideal and work toward it with the courage which will not know when it is beaten, the faith which can stand the shock of repeated disillusion, and the patience which holds on in spite of every set-back.[1]

Such was the spirit of the man who moulded the thought of his own communion and beyond it, as the issues of a World Church began to unfold. It is perhaps fitting that this account of Peake's ecumenical labours should close with a tribute from the pen of the Archbishop of Canterbury (Dr Lang) expressed in a letter written to Mrs Peake following her husband's death:

... We were thrown very closely together for some years in the Conferences which were held, and over which I presided at Lambeth on the great though difficult theme of Christian Union. Of all those who took part in these Conferences he was the one who seemed most anxious, while maintaining his own principles, to understand and sympathize with the point of view of others. Again and again at difficult moments it was his openness of mind and breadth of brotherly sympathy which enabled us to continue. He seemed always to bring into these discussions, not only knowledge and sympathy, but also a quite special loyalty to the Mind of our Lord.

J. T. WILKINSON

[1] *Holborn Review* (1927), p. 511.

A LAYMAN'S TRIBUTE

As my contacts with Dr Peake were personal I shall have to speak more of myself in this appreciation than I would wish; also as he died before Methodist Union was achieved I shall have to refer to Primitive Methodism and its customs. I do it with affection. Although I came to know Dr Peake well in the last years, perhaps anything I have to tell may seem trivial when set alongside our remembrance of him as a great biblical scholar. Yet perhaps I may take comfort as I remember that Boswell, in recording with minuteness of detail particulars of Dr Johnson's conversations, declared that such things are frequently characteristic when they relate to a distinguished man.

It was at the Manchester District Meeting during a week-end at Oldham, the equivalent of the present-day Synod, that I first met Dr Peake. It was the custom to elect to the office of chairman and vice-chairman a minister and a layman respectively, whose duties ended with the close of the session. Such elections were held in high honour by the recipients. Although usually the chairman was a minister and the vice-chairman a layman, occasionally the order was reversed. On this occasion Dr Peake was elected to the chair, and a much esteemed minister became vice-chairman. Dr Peake fulfilled the duties with efficiency and dispatch. Here is a note from my diary, 30th April 1917:

> Afternoon session interesting, but the tone was depressing, the speakers taking a very gloomy view of the condition of the Churches. Dr Peake, however, winding up the conversation, took a more optimistic view of the situation, pointing to the higher ethical standards and other hopeful features of Church life and enterprise. He also reminded us that this is God's work, and spoke of divine resources which, if we were faithful would never fail us.

In Primitive Methodism it was the custom to hold the Ordination Service at the District Meetings and not at the Conference as at present. In this way the ordinand was within easy reach of the circuit and church where he had worshipped, and also of his relatives and friends. Not only was a charge given to the ordinand by a minister, but also a charge to the Church by a layman. It so happened that I was the layman who on that Monday evening gave the charge to the Church. Dr Peake, as Chairman of the District Meeting, presided, and gave the right hand of fellowship. I mention this because after the service he took me on one side and spoke appreciatively of the charge I had given. His words were greatly encouraging. Down the years that followed I often benefited from his encouragements—as did so many young men—and that night a series of conversations began in which Dr Peake quickened my interest in many things, not least in the welfare of the ministry, together with the standard and quality of ministerial training. By his reasoning and even appeal he inspired me to action. If I have been able, even in a small way, to further these interests down the years, I very gratefully and humbly acknowledge my debt to Dr Peake.

At the Hull Conference of 1920 the draft basis for negotiations on Methodist Union was first discussed. Never did Methodist Union come nearer defeat in Primitive Methodism than on that occasion. The opposition put their case brilliantly. The most telling point in the debate was the following. In the course of a clever speech, a northern lawyer said: 'Do you realize that if these proposals are adopted only a minister and never a layman can be President of the United Conference? Do you realize that Dr Peake will never be able to sit in the Presidential Chair?' A tense feeling swept over the Conference Assembly, a measure of the high regard in which Dr Peake was held. The reply came from a later speaker in the debate. 'I yield to none in my regard for Dr Peake. I should like to see him President of the United Conference. I agree that there should be no such limitation in the choice of a President. But when I weigh in the scales this comparatively small matter against the greater issue of Methodist Union, I am compelled to sacrifice, if it is necessary, the lesser for the greater.' Dr Peake himself fully agreed with this remark. In some confusion the Conference adjourned the debate until the following morning, when a compromise was agreed upon and negotiations were allowed to proceed. Although there were always a few opponents, Methodist Union was never again in real danger in Primitive Methodism.

I recall a later Conference when Dr Peake thought that as Primitive Methodists we were pressing our own interest and point of view too strongly, and also that tolerance and charity were lessening. He made a great speech in which he gave us the order of his loyalties. These were as follows—first, to Jesus Christ; second, to the Church Catholic; third, to Methodism; fourth, to Primitive Methodism; fifth, to his own local church. The Church Catholic stood high in his loyalties. His interest in ecumenical movements is well known. I was sitting next to him at the Manchester Conference of 1926. It was usual to read the Minutes which the General Purposes Committee had passed during the year, and if they were 'unticked' they became resolutions of the Conference. One Minute stated that, in the interests of economy, it was recommended that representatives should not be sent to the forthcoming Faith and Order Conference at Lausanne. I called 'tick', which meant that later I could move the amendment or rejection of the Minute. After a moment or two, Dr Peake said how grateful he was that I had given notice, and that he had been so shocked that he failed to call the 'tick' himself. I pressed him to speak to the reversal of the Minute, but with his usual modesty he insisted that I should do so, and should urge that three representatives should be appointed. I did so, Dr Peake seconded the amendment, and Conference agreed. One of the three was Dr Peake himself, and at the Lausanne Conference Sir Henry Lunn, who had not previously met Dr Peake, expressed his delight that Primitive Methodism had sent a man with such a lofty sense of churchmanship.

During the sessions of the Conference one of the things which used to amaze us was the way in which from beginning to end he remained in his place. He must have sat through many hours when the business was of little interest to him. Great was his delight when a reform was adopted whereby all mere formal business in the way of reports and accounts were brought together in one section of the agenda, and moved *en bloc* without speeches, and usually without discussion. Conference, however, could not long be humdrum if you were sitting near to him. He seemed able to extract humour from the most prosaic of subjects, and his comments, which were never unkindly, showed how quickly he saw the amusing side of things. At one Conference when the time-honoured opening hymn was announced, he remarked to me that he always thought 'And are we yet alive' should be sung at the end of Conference rather than at the beginning! He had a delight in funny stories. When voting was proceeding early in one Conference I told him a story that made him laugh heartily. During that Conference at least half a dozen people called me aside to ask if I had heard Dr Peake's latest story, and I heard my own story re-told. Of course I did not 'let on'.

At Manchester University there was a very close friendship between Dr Peake and Professor Samuel Alexander, the philosopher. A friend of mine witnessed the following incident. Professor Alexander was proceeding along Oxford Road on his tricycle and saw Peake walking toward him. When he got within shouting distance, ignoring the busy throng, Alexander called out: 'Peake, I've found God.' When they came together Alexander dismounted, and on the pavement the two men had a long discussion. One would give much for the record of that conversation. I saw Alexander at Peake's funeral, and never have I seen more stricken grief than Alexander showed that day.

In the Committee on Methodist Union Peake had been for ten years a powerful influence—none stood before him. At the first meeting after his passing, we were under a cloud. Never shall I forget the speech in which Dr Scott Lidgett expressed the thoughts of the whole Committee. In fine terms, eloquent and comprehensive, he summarized the splendid contribution Peake had made to the whole Church.

When I look back to my youth and recall the theological outlook, and the sermons to which I listened, I marvel that Peake's coming to Hartley College did not stir up more division and discord. I can remember my own grandfather, Alexander Barlow, who in his youth knew Hugh Bourne, showing distinct uneasiness concerning the new teaching at the College. With Peake's arrival there came a revolution both inside the College and outside it, as many Primitive Methodists became aware for the first time of the new and modern view of the Bible. Why was it that we Primitive Methodists, at that time conservative in theological opinions, were free from any serious heresy-hunts such as occurred in certain other communions? I would claim that it was due in the main to Dr Peake.

No appreciation can omit a reference to his saintliness. He was not only a great scholar but a devout Christian, whose charm and persuasiveness of personality and simple goodness, allayed fears, disarmed suspicion, and won affection. I recall one small confirmation of this. We had met at the College to do him honour, and he was told of an unexpected testimony to his goodness, and one that was not intended for his ears. It was a casual remark of the servant-maid at his home: 'Well of course Dr Peake is a real Christian.' He was surprised and said with some emotion how he valued such a tribute.

I rejoice in every movement of the Spirit whereby men and women are brought into the Kingdom of our Lord. There is a danger, however, that evangelism may be regarded as linked only with a narrow scriptural interpretation. Evangelism is all the better if the emotional appeal can have an intellectual basis; many will be lost to the Kingdom if reason and truth are in any way discounted. It was for the union of scholarship and evangelism that Peake stood, and no one who heard him preach, as he did many years ago at Bury, on 'The Penitent Thief' can ever think of regarding these as in any way to be separated.

Of Arthur Samuel Peake the familiar words are true indeed:

> *His life was gentle; and the elements so mixed in him*
> *That nature might stand up*
> *And say to all the world: 'This was a man.'*

A. B. HILLIS

IMPRESSIONS OF AN EARLY STUDENT

IN view of the fact that it is now over twenty-five years since Dr Peake died, and that therefore many of his contemporaries have long since passed away, the consideration now of the man and his work might seem by this time to be outmoded. Yet it was only a few months ago that I heard on the wireless a tribute to Dr Peake and his pioneer work in the publication of his *Commentary* as a Roman Catholic dignitary sought to commend a similar effort being made by his Church. From such a source and in such a connexion and after so great a lapse of time such reference is of particular significance. From an unsuspected quarter it comes as a token that Dr Peake had a message which made itself felt and which initiated a method which is not outworn. Take yet another type of evidence. Dr Oesterley and Dr Theodore H. Robinson represent denominational affiliations other than those of Dr Peake, but in the volume jointly produced by them, *Hebrew Religion: Its Origin and Development*, there is an inscription: 'Dedicated to the Memory of Arthur S. Peake, Teacher, Scholar, Friend.' The phrase bears witness to the sense of weighty authority, constant freshness in research, and withal the endearing and intimate qualities of this explorer in the realms of sacred learning.

Personally I had the privilege of knowing Dr Peake over many years—from his first coming to Manchester to the time of his death. Attendance at popular lectures given by him on 'The Prophets of Israel' delivered at the Friends' Meeting House in that city brought me as a youth under his spell. Before becoming a candidate for the ministry I had the good fortune to be a member of the Great Western Street Circuit, Manchester, with which Dr Peake was in active association. Frequently I heard him preach and was impressed by his quiet, unassuming but penetrating interpretation of the Word. His rich devotional spirit pervaded every part of the service. One worshipper was heard to say on leaving: 'I would walk ten miles to hear that man pray.' In those days a prayer-meeting always followed the Sunday-evening service, and never once did Dr Peake make a breach in that habit. His conduct of that after-meeting made one recognize how real was his belief in the priesthood of believers and it gave proof of his sensitiveness in seeking to follow the lead of the Spirit in supplication.

Many recollections cluster round Dr Peake in the College. To all freshmen at their first session was handed a set of questions from Dr Peake, the answers to which must have disclosed to him how great was the need of his teaching. But typical of his care and thoroughness was the fact that those papers were returned to each student with discriminating comments which in turn must have revealed how much had to be unlearnt and how many were the gaps in knowledge to be bridged.

In my time Dr Peake dictated his lectures word for word amid a silence only broken by the chiming of the quarters from the clock in the tower, or by an occasional question from the floor of the hall. The lecturer's voice would flow in calm, measured fashion, unhurried, unhasting, never metallic or wooden, but vibrant with the feeling suitable to the theme. Now and again would come a pause, pens would drop, and some remark or the telling of a humorous incident would light up the serious topic in hand. Any attempt at ill-timed interruption would be quietly but effectively scotched, but any pertinent query would receive fitting answer, illuminating and satisfying.

It is difficult to say which of his lectures were most popular. Some on Old Testament Exegesis were apt to be disconcerting. For example, the meaning of Isaiah 1^8 was being dealt with. Was it to be taken as a promise? 'Though your sins be as scarlet they shall be white as snow, though they be red like crimson, they shall be as wool.' Or were the words to be taken as uttered in sarcasm? 'Let them be white as snow.' Or were they couched in a tone of indignation? 'If your sins are as scarlet, how should they be reckoned as snow. If they are red like crimson, how should they be as wool?' The last was declared to give the best sense. As the session broke up that morning one student was heard ruefully to mutter: 'Another sermon gone west!' Not always, however, did the tutor so plainly state his preference. Mostly his method was to state all the possible interpretations of a difficult passage and then leave the verdict to the judgement of the individual student. This again might provoke comment, but in another vein, as when the growl burst forth: 'Why doesn't he tell us just what he himself thinks about this?'

In the Old Testament, however, probably the greatest treasure-trove was found in his elucidation of the message of the prophets and in his portraiture of their character. In the New Testament the massive yet intensely human figure of Paul was made to live and the theology of his experience made palpitatingly real. In Biblical Introduction he was painstaking to a degree, and shirked no difficulty. Any student who worked carefully through those lectures would be well primed for further personal study in the years ahead. Perhaps it was in Biblical Theology that Dr Peake proved himself to have mastered the art of the maxim *Multum in parvo*. In all his utterances indeed there was never a wasted word, but these lectures were as close-packed pemmican.

Always, however, the conviction was borne in upon us that rich wealth lay waiting, not yet shared. Many of us left college hoping to see in the near future a volume from Dr Peake's pen on *Isaiah* (in the *International Critical Commentary*) taking up where Buchanan Gray had left off. Especially did we look forward to what we were sure would be his *magnum opus*, a large volume affording ample scope for adequate treatment of Paulinism. Neither materialized, but as token of what might have been expected, like a nugget of gold came his *Quintessence of Paulinism*. And for the rest, did he not set other minds working and other pens writing, as he brought out his great *Commentary?* And where shall we ever see an index such as that with which he provided it.

As an extra in the course, came his lectures on the History of Doctrine, from which stood out his attempt to guide us in the strange mazes of Gnosticism. Here one was moved by the powerful evidences that the lecturer had immersed himself in the literature of his subject and was imparting first-hand knowledge. How that impression was deepened by reading later his voluminous article on Basilides in the *Encyclopedia of Religion and Ethics*.

Outside the lecture room Dr Peake's influence was persuasive. With a remarkable memory for faces and names he knew every man. He would go out of his way to help any. One day a student approached him, asking how he might have access to some of the books by Continental critics which had been cited in lectures. Within a very short time a ticket for the use of John Rylands Library was forthcoming, along with a list of translations; and this was for one who did not shine in examinations, yet had the virtue of an inquiring mind!

His fame as a biblical critic spread, and often led to misconceptions of his main purpose. A lady once said to him in the College: 'You enjoy this work of analysis, allocating passages to J, E, D, P, and solving the Synoptic problem.' 'No,' he said, 'you have got it wrong. That is only preliminary work.' He urged upon all and sundry that after using all available means to put each portion of the Scriptures in its historic setting, and as far as possible in its chronological succession, there was needed the attuned heart and the listening ear to catch the divine Word breaking through the ancient record. To him revelation and inspiration were supreme realities. Among the many book notices which he wrote for *The Holborn Review* perhaps none was so poignant as an extract which he quoted on the tragic possibility of being well versed in biblical lore, and yet missing its essential touch upon one's own soul.

No one could come into intimate touch with Dr Peake without becoming aware that his was a nature singularly quick to feel the sin and sorrow of suffering humanity. The sight of pain hurt his conscience, and led to his first Hartley Lecture—given in 1904—bearing the title *The Problem of Suffering in the Old Testament*. Re-reading it brings back the quivering emphasis and wistful tone of much of the substance of that valuable work given to us who were in college during the period of its preparation. One can still catch the pathos in the voice that said: 'The problem of pain is of all problems the most baffling to many who wish to accept a theistic view of the universe. Even sin and death are mysteries less oppressive and impenetrable. If sin is a darker evil, pain is the more obscure.' Hence he was at home in the exposition of Job or Hosea or Jeremiah. Others have felt as he did (notably A. B. Davidson, to whose work he often appealed), but it would seem that Dr Peake more than others had reached the serener side of the Cross, for he dwelt in the faith and experience of the New Testament at least as much as, if not more than, in the message of the Old. It meant much to his students that they had in him one with an all-round biblical view.

In the syllabus of the College Literary Society his name regularly appeared, and he paid his audience the compliment of treating them to the best from his wide range of knowledge. From writers of fiction he picked out George Meredith. (In his *Guide to Biblical Study* he said of Dr Salmon: 'His accounts of foreign critics remind one too strongly of George Meredith's Egoist, who in his travels through Europe was engaged in "holding a review of his Maker's grotesques".') Whilst mentioning this phase of his interest in college life, it may be added that he divulged that it had been his custom for years to read aloud daily from the English classics. This doubtless was one secret of the charm of his style, so captivating and convincing.

Between students and the governing body of the College he showed himself a wise and understanding mediator, especially on one outstanding instance of head-on collision between the entire body of students and a luckless principal. The prowess of the Hartley footballers in inter-collegiate matches found in him warmest appreciation, good sportsman as he was. It was also believed that the engagement of varied local talent for college socials by a generous layman owed much to his suggestion.

Outside the College Dr Peake did much for the religious life of Manchester. I recall attending a public meeting organized by the Sunday School Union at which he delivered a striking address that foreshadowed the vigorous lead afterwards given in his book on *Reform in Sunday School Teaching*.

His consuming passion for popularizing Christian truth and defending it against attack caused him readily to accede to the request of Dr J. Hope Moulton to take part in a team of speakers who in 1904 on Sunday afternoons spoke to a crowd averaging about a thousand in number on 'Is Christianity True?' Dr Peake argued on 'Did Jesus rise again?' Without a note, but with well-ordered argument, lucid expression, and compelling force, he dealt with doubts and pressed home the evidence for the crowning miracle. The following year by request in a series on 'What is Christianity?' he gave a searching address on 'The Atonement' which had a powerful effect on believers as well as inquirers. Mention has been made in this paragraph of Dr Peake's speaking without notes. This was his habit in the pulpit as well as on the platform, and about its value as a method he held strong views, though after one popular lecture he confessed to me that it sometimes meant that not so much ground was covered as if manuscript had been used.

The Free Church Council movement had in him a supporter and advocate. For his Presidential Address at the National Council he prepared carefully for the Press, but in delivery when he came to a passage involving judgement on papal claims he was stirred to improvise what became known as his famous 'IF' passage.

Religious instruction in day-schools naturally was to him a matter of deep moment and he was early engaged in co-operation with others in the pioneering of an Agreed Syllabus for Religious Instruction.

For his own denomination Dr Peake toiled unceasingly. At Ministerial Associations (especially the one which served the Manchester and Liverpool area) he was a frequent contributor. As editor of the *Holborn Review* he kept ministers in constant touch with the trends of biblical scholarship. Publishers vied with one another in sending to him books for signed review, but in periodical surveys he made his own selection from books which he had himself discovered and used and could commend. These surveys of English and foreign work were invaluable and lent distinction to the quarterly.

During his editorship there were springing up throughout the Church Study Circles of old students who felt the continuing impact of the inspiration they had received at College, and wished to have the benefit of group discussion on biblical, theological, social, and literary matters. I ventured to suggest to Dr Peake that a section of the *Review* might be devoted to the interests of this spontaneous movement. This was evidently after his own heart, and he at once concurred. On subjects being named to him he would allocate a space and use his influence to secure experts to write articles giving groundwork for study and discussion. Reports of the groups were provided quarterly, and these helped to link them up with one another and to afford further incentive.

In denominational committees and at the annual Conference Dr Peake brought to bear his sound judgement and far-seeing idealism. There flashes to my mind the scene on one drowsy summer afternoon when the Conference agenda had an item dealing with the conception of a World Church, which Sir Henry Lunn was seeking to foster by gatherings abroad of Church leaders from time to time. Dr Peake was spokesman and soon he had the Conference fully awake and stirred, as with the vision of a prophet he portrayed the healing of the rent robe of unity.

In private correspondence I once had with him he hinted at attempts that were being made to lure him from Primitive Methodism, and to provide for him what many admirers felt would be a more worthy setting for his brilliant gifts. But though financial pressure and spells of ill-health and other factors might have given him good ground for yielding to these appeals, yet right to the very end he maintained his complete loyalty and unflinching attachment to the Church into which he had been born. In this commemorative volume it is fitting that this should be stressed. Never in our midst was there a more shining example of utter self-forgetfulness and complete sacrifice to a sacred and life-long task, the training of ministers for our Church.

Thus, in the Providence of God, in the course of long years at College he led ministers, and through them thousands of Primitive Methodists, into appropriation of a setting of biblical truth far wider that that which had been conceived in their beginnings and all this without any diminution of evangelistic fervour.

And it should be remembered this was done by one who was not himself a minister, though a son of the manse. Never had human hands of ordination been laid upon him. He to whom we all owed so much was a layman. But every minister gratefully recognized in him the signs of divine commission and the sure and certain tokens of efficacious grace. If anyone outside our borders had had the effrontery to attribute the inspiration that flowed from him, a layman, to uncovenanted mercies, that notion would have been at once repudiated by those who had known his ministry.

Supremely Arthur Samuel Peake was a Man of God, a Messenger of the Word. The torch he lit and bore has come down to us, and we best honour him as we let its light brightly shine amid the darkness still around us.

W. E. FARNDALE

IN THE STUDY

I HAVE been asked to write on 'Dr Peake in his study'. I do so with a great deal of hesitation, being accustomed to having articles dictated to me, not to writing them. But having spent nearly twenty-five very happy years in Dr Peake's study, perhaps I ought to make an attempt to comply with the request.

It was in November 1904 that I first made Dr Peake's acquaintance, when he asked me to go to see him at his house. He explained to me the nature of his work and what he would like me to do, adding that he wasn't wanting a machine. Among other things he asked me if I should mind spring-cleaning his books, as he liked them handled by people who knew how to treat them. He said he had always hesitated to employ a lady, as he wouldn't like to send her out in bad weather, and it was necessary sometimes for his secretary to go to town or to the bank. While we were talking a little boy opened the door. Seeing a stranger there he paused for a moment. This was my first introduction to his eldest son, who as a little child always had a great affection for and implicit trust in his father. He used to spend quite a lot of time in the study, sitting on his father's knee while he was dictating.

Dr Peake showed me his study. There was a number of papers lying about, and he said that perhaps I should be able to keep it tidier for him. I suggested that some people would rather not have their papers disturbed. He said he did not mind, so long as it was the right person who did it. Dr Peake's study was never too tidy for work. Sometimes after he had been away for a day or two he would gaze on it with satisfaction on his return, but the empty spaces on the desks would be quickly filled up with letters, books, and papers.

There is no need for me to speak of the immense amount of work Dr Peake got through; all his friends knew what a great worker he was, though outsiders would sometimes take a different view. We used to work in the garden sometimes at Freshfield when the weather was nice. I remember one hot summer afternoon when Dr Peake was lying in the garden dictating, I had just got up to fetch a book from the study when the postman came along with some letters. He handed them to Dr Peake with the remark: 'I wish I'd got your job.'

Now and then Dr Peake used to receive anonymous letters, which would cause him a good deal of amusement. I quote from one that is many years old: 'What bit of learning you have is some old dry Church history that you got from other men's labours. . . . It is clear that Methodism is made use of for some to have an idle life. . . . Woe to the man that makes religion a trading concern for an easy life.' One winter session Dr Peake had as many as twenty-one lectures in the week, for in addition to lecturing at Hartley, Lancashire and the United Methodist Colleges, and at the University, he had consented to give a course of lectures in Liverpool. After a heavy day's lecturing he would settle down to work in his study in the evening, where a lot of correspondence would be waiting, or there would be articles or reviews that had to be written. At first I used to go to his house for half a day, but whether it was morning, afternoon or evening would depend largely on the time he was lecturing; if he was specially busy I should be there both morning and evening. Unless Dr Peake was away from home I was generally kept busier in the vacations than in term time.

Dr Peake always opened his own letters, and preferred to dictate the replies, and with the exception of formal invitations and letters asking for subscriptions (when he would tell me what to send) he seldom handed anything over to me to deal with myself. Though he told me at the beginning that much of his correspondence was of a private nature and he would want me to regard it as such, if he received a letter the contents of which he thought the writer would prefer no one else to become acquainted with, the reply would either be dictated in language which would convey nothing to me, or a letter would be sent in his own handwriting, however busy he might be. Letters containing invitations to preach or lecture would come in very frequently. The average man would have turned these over to his secretary, telling her to reply in the negative, but when Dr Peake had to decline these invitations, as he usually had, he would dictate a carefully worded letter, explaining why he was unable to accept. Had he accepted all the invitations he received he might have been away every Sunday in the year. But he made a point of spending his week-ends at home.

I soon realized what a very busy man Dr Peake was, but what

impressed me even more than his capacity for work was his wonderful capacity for kindness, which he lavished not only on his family and those who worked for him, but on everyone with whom he came in contact, either personally or through correspondence. His kindness, courtesy, and perfect consideration for others were often revealed in his letters. One of the first people I had to write to was the gardener whom he was in the habit of employing. A poor man had come along with a tale of woe asking for work, and Dr Peake had given him something to do in the garden, and told him he could come again the next day. Thinking that his regular gardener might pass that way and feel upset at seeing someone else at work there, he asked me to send him a note explaining the situation. He often received letters asking for financial help. I don't think this was ever refused, except when the applicant turned out to be a scoundrel. Once when I ventured to suggest to Dr Peake that he was being imposed on, he said he would rather help a good many undeserving cases than miss one genuine case where he could really be of service, and if there was any doubt he always gave other people the benefit of it. His readiness to help his boys in schemes and experiments which would not have appealed to him at all personally may be illustrated by a sentence from one of their letters: 'Your letter put new life into me. I knew you would help me all you could.'

Letters asking for advice on theological subjects or with reference to the purchase of books or the study of them always received careful attention. If by chance there was a letter of complaint to be written it would be so admirably worded that one would hardly recognize that any fault was being found, but Dr Peake would usually succeed in getting the matter that needed attention put right without giving offence or hurting anyone's feelings. It is a great regret to me now that we did not keep duplicates of all the letters that were written, but Dr Peake did not think it necessary except in a few cases where he might want them for reference, though he always liked duplicates taken of book MSS, articles of reviews, in case they went astray in the post or were lost by some careless printer, which did happen occasionally. Dr Peake must have given great pleasure by many of the letters he wrote, if the recipients got as much pleasure out of reading them as I did out of writing them. He often received letters from old students expressing their gratitude and appreciation for the influence he had

had on their lives. Book parcels were always opened with keen interest, whether they were books he had ordered or books that had come for review. Many came for the *Holborn Review* and some for the *Times Literary Supplement*. If three or four parcels arrived at once I should be allowed to cut the string and clear away the packing, but he always liked to discover what was in the parcels himself; he would often make a guess at what they contained before opening them.

Dr Peake had a second study at the top of the house, with bookshelves all round. He spent most of his time in the downstairs study, but if he was at work on a commentary he preferred to write this upstairs, so that he could leave his work on the desk with the books he needed to consult open around it, and he would go up there when he could spare an hour or two from his regular work. His commentary on Jeremiah was written in this way entirely with his own hand, and typed out afterwards, though he was in the habit of dictating his other books. At the time he was taken ill the desk in the upstairs study was covered with the books he was using in preparation for his commentary on Isaiah for the *International Critical Commentaries*. He had been working on this a good deal in the early part of July 1929, and had been hoping to get forward with it very considerably during the summer vacation.

In the early days I used to take down the letters and articles in shorthand, but for many years Dr Peake dictated straight to the typewriter. This saved a good deal of time, and had the advantage that he was able to read what he had written as he went along. In the winter I used to work the typewriter on a revolving chair by the fire, which could be twisted round to him at any moment. Dr Peake always believed in trying new things, and while he was at Wellington Road he bought a dictaphone, thinking it would be very convenient if he could dictate when I was not there. But this was not a great success—perhaps because I never got into the way of using it properly—and it was never used after we went to Freshfield, because it worked by electricity and there was none in the Freshfield house.

Mrs Peake and the boys were never well in Manchester in the wintertime. The doctor thought that if the boys could go to live by the sea for a few years it might establish their health. So in 1912 they took a house at Freshfield near Southport. Here Dr

IN THE STUDY

Peake had a large, beautiful study with a south aspect; he always liked a sunny room and so did I, but no room that Dr Peake was in was ever without sunshine. Another study at the top of the house accommodated the surplus books and left plenty of room for additions. Unfortunately Dr Peake had not much time to spend in this nice study except at the week-ends and in vacation time. At first he used to travel to and from Manchester every day he had engagements there, but he found this very taxing and especially trying in the wintertime when he frequently got bad coughs. Later he was persuaded to stay at Hartley College, and as a rule came into Manchester on Monday afternoon and returned on Thursday afternoon or evening, though often he would not be able to return till Friday, and sometimes meetings or committees kept him in Manchester until Saturday.

It was very much more difficult for Dr Peake to do his work under these conditions than when he was living in Manchester, but he made the best of it, as he did of everything, and did not trouble about himself as long as his family were well and happy, and it was possible for him to carry on his work. It meant that for several days in the week he was away from his library; review books and other material for work had to be carried backwards and forwards a good deal. Catching and missing trains probably took less out of him than it would have done out of most people, though he must have wasted many an hour on Liverpool Station, because the connexions were bad. If I was with him and we just missed the train by half a second, having the barrier shut in our faces, I used to feel very indignant, but he always took it very philosophically, and would put in the twenty minutes or half-hour we had to wait looking at the book-stall, and perhaps buying a detective story or two. He was glad to settle down at home for a few weeks when lectures were over, though even then he would sometimes have to come into Manchester for meetings or committees which he was too conscientious to cut. I used to spend week-ends at Freshfield sometimes when Dr Peake was specially busy, though usually it was in vacation time that I was there. It was always a real pleasure to me to go down, both to see Mrs Peake and the boys and to help Dr Peake in his spacious study where there was plenty of room for the work, and where the books were shown to advantage.

One of the reasons why Dr Peake appreciated having a larger

study was that he was able to have the cabinet in it, which had been given him by the students of Hartley College after he had been there ten years. He greatly valued this, and often pointed it out to visitors with much pleasure. His study in Wellington Road had been too small to accommodate it, so it had had to go in the drawing-room. We used to work at times in the summer-house that was given to Dr Peake by the Hartley College students after he had been there twenty-one years. The family also made very good use of this.

On the occasion of the celebrations of the twenty-first year of his tutorship at Hartley College on 11th June 1914, Dr Peake's portrait[1] and the stained-glass windows which Sir William Hartley had put into the College Chapel were unveiled. Though Dr Peake was extra busy through my being ill, he found time to write letters of thanks to everyone who had contributed to make the day a success, including the cook at Hartley College.

Generally speaking Dr Peake worked easily, and seldom made any drastic alterations in what he dictated, though occasionally he would begin an article over again if he was not satisfied with it. He was not unduly disturbed if people came into the room while he was working, though latterly if he was interrupted he found it more difficult to pick up his threads again, especially if he was dictating anything that required concentration. I remember one morning at Freshfield, when visitors were staying there, we had so many interruptions that I began to make a list. In just over an hour they amounted to seventeen. One of the intruders was Dr Peake's little nephew (then six) who came running in saying he just wanted a rock in uncle's rocking-chair. Many men would have been exasperated at being disturbed so often, but Dr Peake simply said we must make the most of our time when they had all gone out. This was of course an exceptional day; we were not usually disturbed so frequently. But I remember on another occasion (possibly during a coal shortage) his eldest son could not do his lessons with the two younger boys in the room, so they had to come into the study and Dr Peake had to try to dictate while they were running their trains across the floor. He was the most patient as well as the most kind-hearted and self-sacrificing man I have ever met. He could be absolutely relied on, and if he had promised a book or article to the publishers by a definite date he

---

[1] This is reproduced as frontispiece to the present volume.—Ed.

would work extra late in the evening or on into the morning to complete it. When he was writing his New Testament Introduction he had to finish dictating it lying on the sofa, and afterwards he had rather a serious attack of brain-fag, and had to take a month's rest. He was just as considerate and easy to work for when he was not feeling well. I once remarked that illness did not make him cross and irritable as it did so many people, and he replied that it was surely bad enough to be ill oneself without making other people ill.

It was a great upheaval when Dr Peake had to return to Manchester in 1920. He had no choice of house, as it was at a time when there was scarcely a house to be got, and he thought he was fortunate to have got one in Whalley Range so near the College. But as it was so much smaller than the one he had left and would not take several of the book-shelves, many of his books had to go to his room at the University or at Hartley College. It took a long while to get the books arranged again. In spite of the fact that the study at Albert Road never looked tidy, Dr Peake was really very methodical. He usually had a good many pieces of work on hand at once, and he had several nests of drawers which varied in size containing from three to eight drawers. Here we used to keep the work that was in progress, otherwise it would have got buried on the desk. These drawers were added to from time to time, till we had about fourteen sets. Two or three drawers were devoted to the *Holborn Review*, one to the Free Church Council, one to the *Times Literary Supplement*, one to 'Lambeth', others to lecture notes and several to letters. I had one drawer labelled 'Biography'. Several friends used to express the wish that Dr Peake would write an autobiography, and I often tried to persuade him to do this, but he always felt he had more important work waiting to be done. I made the suggestion that all the time that was devoted to work after ten in the evening might be utilized for this purpose, but I could not get Dr Peake to consent even to this. Twice when we were away on holiday he did spend a little time dictating some incidents of his childhood, but he impressed on me that the manuscript was never to go into print as it was.

I should like to add a word about holidays, because I think some people are under the impression that Dr Peake could not enjoy a holiday. I can say with conviction that this was quite a mistake, for having spent many happy holidays with him and his family, I have had some opportunity of judging. He was not fond of long journeys or slow trains, but would put up with them for the sake of others or if there was some particular object in view, as for instance when he went abroad. But he enjoyed driving or motoring, and also walking if the distance was not too great, though long walks always tired him. But I think the chief enjoyment he got out of a holiday consisted in the knowledge that he was giving pleasure to others. I never enjoyed any holidays so much as those spent with Dr Peake. He would study everyone's individual tastes and what they wanted to do, and was extraordinarily generous, as indeed he was on every occasion. Work often went with us, though not always, but this did not mean that Dr Peake was not having any holiday. He usually packed a box of books if he were going for any time; some of them would be for work, some would be detective stories, and some would be for other people to read. The index to his book on *The Bible* was largely done in Cornwall, and the index to the *Commentary* was started at Goathland. We never stayed in to work on fine days, but if there was a thoroughly wet day it was a satisfaction to Dr Peake to feel that it need not be wasted, and we used to settle down to work sometimes after supper.

From the first Dr Peake always made me feel that I had a share in his work. He was most appreciative of everything that was done for him, and very lenient if one made mistakes. The wish that he expressed when first I went to him that I might like the work was amply fulfilled. The pleasure in it increased as the years went on. No one ever had a kinder friend or more considerate employer than I had in Dr Peake. It may interest some readers to know that almost the last piece of work he had undertaken to do was an article for the *Dictionnaire Encyclopedique de la Bible*, which Prof. Westphal was editing. It was to have been ready by 1st February 1930, and then translated into French. The editor was delighted with his promise to do it, and wrote: 'I will not dwell upon the kind words which you express in your letter with regard to me, but I wish to tell you what a great joy your acceptance is for me because of the manner in which your thought corresponds with mine from the scientific as well as the spiritual point of view.' It is a tragedy that so much of Dr Peake's work was to be left undone.

ELSIE CANN

IN THE FAMILY CIRCLE

THE home into which my father, Arthur Samuel Peake, was born both coloured and conditioned much that he said. Indeed it would be interesting to speculate what might have happened had his early background been secular instead of sacred, had his abode been fixed instead of subject to constant change, or had he himself been an only child instead of one in a family of seven. Had his mother, for whom he always felt the deepest and most tender affection, not died at the early age of thirty-nine, when he himself was but a boy of nine, would he have passed more easily and securely through the turbulent days of adolescence and early manhood? Or had his elder sister, Alice, whose extraordinary precocity was a source of amazement to all who knew her, and upon whom her father had pinned his highest hopes, not been suddenly taken at the slender age of three, would she have outshone him in later years, and wrested from him some of the laurels he was destined to win?

But speculation, though interesting and not without its value, can hardly be decisive. In so far as it is possible for one person to acquire gifts and graces from another, it would probably be true to say that Arthur received from his father his great love for the Methodist Church, his strong sense of justice and fair play, and, above all, his ever-deepening conviction that while the root and essence of religion are to be found in fellowship with the Unseen, religion itself must always find outlet and expression in the practical conduct of everyday life. His younger sister, Emily, was the inseparable companion of his early years, and as he would proudly say his 'first pupil'. It was largely upon her character and that of his mother that his own high conception of womanhood was modelled. His elder brother, George, was a particularly fine character, exceptionally considerate by nature and without any trace of envy in his disposition. For many years Arthur found in him a constant example and inspiration. Though fourteen years separated him from his youngest brother, William, no one could have watched an elder brother's progress with greater pride than William watched his. Later in life it was one of his special joys to have Arthur's books beautifully bound in leather.

Taken all in all, it was a very happy fellowship, marked by plain living and high thinking. On his father's normal stipend of £88 a year extravagance was out of the question, and at the table it was not so much a case of jam and butter as of butter or jam. What a day it must have been when Arthur heard the news that he had won a Close Scholarship to St John's College, Oxford, consisting of £100 a year for five years! To this, too, was added an Exhibition of £55 a year for four years from his school at Coventry.

And now for nine wonderful years Oxford was to cast her magic spell over him. Yet he never forgot those whose circumstances were less fortunate than his own. Had Christ been living on earth, he declared, He would have been an Oxford socialist, and he even contemplated taking Orders in the Church of England that he might devote his life to working in the slums of London. But in reality he was too deeply rooted in the Methodist tradition ever to have forsaken the Church of his fathers, or to have kicked down the ladder by which he himself had climbed up. Though he owed an incalculable debt to such teachers as Snow, Cheyne, Sanday, Fairbairn, and Hatch, and though a Fellowship at Merton provided him with a beautiful suite of rooms and the sum of £200 a year for seven years, he became increasingly convinced that his call was to the teaching of theology, and that the Church that must claim his allegiance was the Church in which he himself had been nurtured and nourished. Over three years after he had gone up to Oxford, and less than four years before he received his Fellowship from Merton, he wrote these very significant lines to his friend, Willie Meredith: 'It was for Theology that I was born, and I am learning to walk and feel my feet. There are few things which give more perfect pleasure than the consciousness of increasing power.' It was at Oxford that he preached his first sermon in the little village chapel at Murcott in the Oxford Primitive Methodist Circuit on the first Sunday in March 1884. It was in this ancient city he met and married Harriet Mary Sillman, my quiet and retiring mother who shared his home for thirty-seven years, and through whose self-sacrifice his work was made possible. And it was here that he received his call, made feasible by the generosity of the late Sir William Hartley, to become tutor at Hartley College, Manchester.

Christian theology down the centuries swings between Greek and Hebrew poles. My father was essentially a Hebraist. For him the call of duty meant infinitely more than the call of beauty. Had anybody ever challenged him with not loving Nature he would have replied, with Robert Browning, 'Yes, I do, but I love men and women more.' Here, I believe, lay a fundamental difference in outlook between my father and my mother. Though on any question of ultimate importance my mother would have come down, and come down quite definitely, on the side of duty, she would have found it very much harder to forsake the call of beauty. If both of them were feeling depressed in spirit, a few days in the Lake District would turn my mother into a totally different woman; they never had the same effect upon my father. Though he would always call for silence from his children when the train passed through the Shropshire hills, with the remark, 'I knew what beautiful scenery was when I was a boy', his deepest consolation would be found in the case of theological books that he had taken with him. They, rather than the glories of Nature, were his true companions. His last words to me, when he lay dying in the Royal Infirmary at Manchester, were to ask how soon he would be back at his work again. My father could leave Oxford without any deep pangs of regret; my mother couldn't. My father was so completely absorbed by the thought of training men for the Primitive Methodist Ministry that the privilege of doing so outshone everything else; my mother, while appreciating this, found it almost incomprehensible that anybody could exchange the rare and unique loveliness of Oxford for the smoke and dirt of Manchester.

Others who are much more qualified to do so have told of my father's work at Hartley College and at the University of Manchester, and of his contributions to biblical scholarship. My concern is with the family circle. What was he like in the home? How did he impress those with whom he lived and worked for twenty-four hours in the day?

I think that my mother's remark to me after the funeral was over, that the strength had gone out of her life, is perhaps the best summary I could offer. Though not always enjoying the best of health, he was essentially a strong man. His convictions were strong. His friendships stood the test of time. His devotion to Christ and His Church was unshakable. He had a character and a personality upon which weaker vessels could lean. At a time of crisis he was like a strong fortress and a haven of refuge. Though he hated the idea that his pupils might ever become gramophone records of himself, such was the strength of his personality that they often found it difficult to avoid the very thing from which he was most anxious that they should escape. His aim was never to produce weak imitations, but always to liberate and develop the individual powers of those whom he taught.

He was a tremendous worker. Probably there was no part of the Bible that he quoted to us more often when we were growing children than the well-known passage about the ant and the sluggard. 'Whatever thy hand findeth to do, do it with all thy might', was one of his favourite sayings. Well do I remember a day when he came home, his face wreathed in smiles, because Sir James Frazer, the author of the *Golden Bough*, had just told him that he was on holiday, since he was working merely eight hours a day instead of his usual sixteen. He loved the story of the American editor who wrote one article with his right hand, another article with his left hand, dictated a third article to his secretary, and then, in order that no part of him might remain inactive, rocked the cradle with his feet. How he would chuckle over the limerick which he composed for himself when he was President of the Primitive Methodist University Union and which ran,

> *A conceited Professor called Peake*
> *Did twelve months' work in a week,*
>   *When they said 'You will rue it,*
>   *If you will overdo it'*
> *He replied: 'Don't you know that I'm PEAKE!!!'*

As a general rule, my father would be in his study and at work by nine o'clock. Unless lectures at Hartley College or the University, of which he was sometimes giving as many as twenty-one in a week, called him forth, he would frequently remain there till midnight, merely emerging for his meals. He loved his work and literally lived for it.

He was not concerned with being a finished stylist. Time, he would declare, was far too precious to be spent in polishing up paragraphs; the all-important thing was to get the paragraphs produced, and to see that they were correct. Nor did he feel that his work should be limited in its appeal to those who were scholars like himself. On the contrary he laboured incessantly to bring the fruits of scholarship into the homes of all who would receive it. Although he liked to feel that his commentaries on Job, Jeremiah, and Hebrews in the *Century Bible* had done something to raise the standard of scholarship in that somewhat unequal series, he found far greater joy in laying his knowledge at the feet of the masses, in the editing of his *Commentary* or in the publication of his *Christianity, its Nature and its Truth*. Indeed he disagreed strongly with those who would dedicate all their scholarship to the furtherance of scholarship, as though that were a laudable end in itself.

Perhaps it was for this very reason that the intricacies of scholarship never marred the simplicity of his heart. To the very roots of his being he was a lover of simple things. His tastes in food, in dress, and in worship were all simple. A plate of ham and broad beans, he would say, was a meal fit for a king, and there was none that he himself enjoyed better. The spectacle of an overdressed woman, he would declare, was enough to make him 'squirm', and the sight of a boy togged up in Eton clothes always reminded him of a dressed-up monkey. The more public worship aimed at simplicity, in hymn, in prayer, and in sermon, the more highly did he rate its value. After a congregation had struggled manfully through an intricate chant, vainly endeavouring to get as many words on to one note as possible, or after a choir had murdered an anthem that was above the heads of most of the people, he would want to know what any body of worshippers could desire better than the sublime simplicities of 'Jesu, Lover of my soul' or 'When I survey the wondrous cross'. It caused him real distress if, after a preacher had taken great pains to state profound truths in simple terms, somebody set him down as lower in intelligence than one who had captured his congregation with long words and high-sounding phrases.

Yet he was no stranger to brilliance. He delighted in brilliant conversation and loved to take part in it. One of his happiest recollections was the Senior Common Room at Merton with its band of illustrious talkers. Both in the home and elsewhere he could 'hold the floor'. On one occasion he and I paid a visit to the home of an Anglican vicar in a small Devonshire village. During the evening the vicar scarcely opened his mouth, but sat with open eyes and ears as my father poured out the treasures of his mind and heart. As we walked down the garden path my father turned to me and said, somewhat to my quiet amusement, 'An unusually intelligent man, that vicar!' Yet the incident is more significant than might appear. Very often I have been tempted to compare my father, even if at a long distance, with the great Dutch scholar, Desiderius Erasmus, whom he resembled so closely at so many points, and not least in his ability to take complete command of a room full of people. P. S. Allen, in the single lecture that brought him by telegram the very rare distinction of an honorary doctorate from the University of Leiden, says:

'In a company of talkers there is usually someone who takes the lead, whose pre-eminence once established is conceded without a struggle by others who are content to listen to what they cannot emulate. . . . From the testimony of those who knew Erasmus, it seems that wherever he went, in whatever company he found himself, he could, if he wished, assume control of the conversation and enthral his listeners.'

If my comparison seems far-fetched, may I quote some words from a letter which the Archbishop of Canterbury, Dr Cosmo Lang, wrote to my mother on the very day of my father's funeral, and which she herself valued above every other tribute she received:

We were, as you know, thrown very closely together for some years in the Conferences which were held, and over which I presided at Lambeth on the great though difficult theme of Christian Union. Of all those who took part in these conferences he was the one who seemed most anxious, while maintaining his own principles, to understand and sympathize with the point of view of others. Again and again at difficult moments it was his openness of mind and breadth of brotherly sympathy which enabled us to continue. He seemed always to bring into these discussions, not only knowledge and sympathy, but also a quite special loyalty to the Mind of our Lord.

But the most precious memories of my father, which twenty-five years have done nothing to dim, are those which centre in his goodness, his kindness, and his loyalty. He was a good man. Believing that Jesus would never have considered it safe to say 'Our Father' had He not added the further words 'Hallowed Be Thy Name', he gave to such words as Honour, Duty, and Reverence, spelt in each case with a capital letter, their right and lawful place. The respect he commanded from others was in no small measure due to the simple fact that they knew that their trust in him would never be put to shame. He was a kind man. Convinced that cruelty was the greatest of all sins, he practised the great art of considerateness in all his dealings. His secretary, Miss Elsie Cann, who served him for nearly twenty-five years with unfailing devotion, was not far from the truth when she referred to him as the 'most kind-hearted man' she had ever met. But, above all, he was a loyal man. Loyal to his Maker in the first instance, he knew how to be loyal to all his friends, and they were many. Even those who had no claim upon him whatever discovered that of his faithfulness there was no end.

Once at the breakfast table, when I was quite a young man, he turned to me and said, 'You will never find so much loyalty in the world that you can ever afford to neglect any.' What I had said or done to call forth the remark I have now no idea. But the remark has lived with me all down the years both as the foundation symbol of his life and as a guiding star for my own.

LESLIE S. PEAKE

PART II

EXCERPTS FROM THE WRITINGS
A. S. PEAKE

I—CRITICAL

THE LEGITIMACY AND NECESSITY OF BIBLICAL CRITICISM

THE very nature of the Bible makes criticism not only legitimate but imperative. This will be best appreciated if we ask ourselves what kind of a book we should have expected the Bible to be, supposing that we had no knowledge of the Bible we actually possess. We should naturally have expected in the first place that it would be a compendium of religious truth. It should expound the nature of God and of man, the relations between them, the rectification of the abnormal tendencies in human nature, and similar topics in a clear and orderly manner; in other words, it should present us with a system of doctrine. Further, it would naturally be consulted for a perfect system of conduct; in other words, it should be a treatise on morality. We might, perhaps, further expect it not only to direct our thought concerning Divine things and control our conduct, but to stimulate the religious emotion. But it is quite clear that such a book would be very different from the Bible we actually possess. For the Bible is neither a treatise on Systematic Theology, nor a handbook on Ethics, nor yet a manual of devotion. It is true that it contains more teaching on Theology than any system of dogmatics has been able to incorporate, and a mass of moral teaching that no moralist has exhausted. For devotional reading it is unrivalled in its power to lift the soul into immediate and unhindered fellowship with God. Yet it possesses all these great qualities in virtue of the fact that primarily it is something else.

If we examine it, apart from any theory, we are struck at the outset by the large proportion of history or narrative, in much of which religion seems to hold a subordinate place. Often it is the development of external events, wars, alliances, rebellions, and other concerns of the statesman. Sometimes it is a series of anecdotes which would not suggest a spiritual significance to us if we met them in other literature. The historians are invaluable in that they exhibit to us the course of Israel's political fortunes, they give us a firm skeleton of fact, but for the flesh and blood and breath of life we have to turn mainly to prophet and poet. The prophets are not engrossed with the far-away past or the distant future, but stand face to face with their contemporaries, dealing closely with their actual life, testing their diplomacy and administration of justice by their exalted social and political ideals, seeking to rectify their relation to God and conduct to their fellow-men. Again in the Wisdom literature of the Old Testament, we have the problems of life discussed, as in Job, or its duties enforced, as in Proverbs. In the Psalms we have the expression of religious experience, often of marvellous depth and range. There is much that is parallel in the New Testament. Here also we have narrative books, describing the life, the teaching, the death, the resurrection of Jesus, and the growth of the early Church. But we also have the Epistles, in which we may see the counterpart to the prophetic literature of the Old Testament. They deal with the urgent present and its problems; even where speculation takes its boldest flight it is that some commonplace duty may be enforced, some problem of conduct grow clear under an intenser light. Now all this means that revelation is a process in history. It is exquisitely fitted to the concrete reality; is no body of abstract propositions, but everywhere intimately associated with life. Its lack of system may perplex us when we first observe it, but when we come to reflect on it, we realize how natural it is for a literature which is a transcript of life to be so incidental.

But, if revelation is mediated through history, we must understand the history in order that we may know the revelation. To gain the greatest good from the Bible we must place ourselves in line with the main stream of it. If we open the writings of a prophet we read words addressed to his own time with its special conditions and peculiar needs. The value of the message, when originally uttered, depended largely on its close applicability to the circumstances with which it dealt. Hence there is often a local and temporal element in Scripture, which must be allowed for if we are to appropriate its permanent message. We must go behind the special application and reach the universal principles applied if we are to reapply those principles to our own wholly different conditions. But we cannot do this without knowing the conditions to which the application is made. It is not too much to say that, for want of this historical study, a large part of the Old Testament

LEGITIMACY AND NECESSITY OF BIBLICAL CRITICISM 85

and some things in the New have been a sealed book to most readers of the Bible. It is true that much in the Bible is not of special application, but is the utterance of the universal and the eternal. But while such passages speak immediately to the heart and are independent of circumstances of time or place, much is lost through failure to understand the historical conditions in which the word first came to the men who heard it. Since the fortunes of Israel changed much from time to time, a book may have quite a different light cast upon it according as its composition is placed in one period or another. Thus questions of date and authorship are of importance for the true interpretation. So also is the determination of the structure of individual books. It will clearly make a great difference to the interpretation of a book if the whole of it is judged to belong to a single period and to one author, or if pieces of different periods and by different authors have been incorporated in it. There is another matter of importance. Christians see in the Religion of Israel a Divinely-ordered preparation for Christianity. But if we have in the Old Testament a progressive revelation leading up to Christ, we need to place its documents in the true order if we are to understand the course which the development took.

But if the Bible is to be studied historically, criticism is indispensable. The history is enshrined in documents, and these documents must be dated and analysed that we may fit each into its proper place in the onward march of God's self-revelation. It is criticism alone that can answer questions as to time and place, circumstances of origin or the composite authorship of the documents. No modern historian would write a history until he had examined by the best methods of scientific criticism the documents from which his narrative was drawn, and there is no reason why sacred history should be deprived of the great advantage derived from critical examination of the sources. It has pleased God to give us the Bible in such a form as to make criticism of it essential if we are truly to understand it in all its fullness and depth of meaning. It is a perpetual challenge to all the qualities of mind and heart, rewarding those most richly who lavish the most loving study upon it, and count no tedious toil too arduous that they may more truly understand by what way God has given it to us.

He who seeks to understand the Bible must recognize that the contribution made by criticism is not the last word upon Scripture. Room must be made for it in the full-orbed theory of the Bible which it is our aim to secure, but it is not competent to give us our ultimate conception of it. There are many factors beside the critical factor which must be taken into account by all who would seek to form a theory of Scripture which shall be in harmony, not with human fancies or with ecclesiastical tradition, but with the Divine fact. But we must not for that reason invert the true order of things and impose the shackles of a preconceived theory on the freedom of critical research.

THE PERMANENT RESULTS OF BIBLICAL CRITICISM

THE nineteenth century was pre-eminently the era of criticism. The critical and historical method was not wholly new even as applied to the sacred literature of Christendom; but it was exercised with unprecedented thoroughness, with detachment from dogmatic control, with instruments of finer and finer precision, handled with a dexterity becoming ever more skilled by practice. No tradition was too sacred for relentless investigation, no belief too cherished to claim exemption from challenge. The process naturally evoked anger and violence, pain and dismay, among those who felt that the critic's knife cut at the very vitals of their religion. But through fierce storms of resentment or clouds of misrepresentation the critic followed the star that he might find his way to Bethlehem and bring his gifts and his worship to the shrine of Truth. For if we may rightly deplore the iconoclastic temper which was too often shown and the new dogmatism which guided his quest and prejudiced his results, it is the barest justice to admit that the critical movement was animated above all by a sincere desire to discover truth. When it was true to its own principles it was free from animus of every kind, it went its own way of impartial inquiry, indifferent whether it helped or hindered the cause of faith. And justly, for if investigation is to be scientific it must be free and not deliberately conducted to reach a given goal. Yet it must not be forgotten that criticism is a special science and while it must be granted autonomy within its own domain, we have to check and combine its results with the results of other lines of inquiry before we reach that complete rounded view in which a due place is accorded to all the facts of which account must be taken.

The wrath and dismay which criticism occasioned were largely due to its negative aspect and the uncertainty in which everything seemed to be involved. Whether it was in the Lower Criticism which sought to restore the true text of Scripture; or the Higher Criticism which attempted to determine the problems of date and authorship, to analyse composite documents into the elements of which they were composed and thus go behind the literature we possess to its sources; or Historical Criticism which estimated first the qualities of the historians and their qualifications for their task and then appraised the historical worth of the documents themselves; there was always a sense of uneasiness aroused by the mere fact that so much which had seemed secure now appeared unsettled. It was as if the solid rock was changing into a quaking morass. The text of Scripture for which infallibility had so often been claimed, was shown to be subject in multitudes of instances to serious uncertainties. Many books were denied to the authors to whom tradition had assigned them, and what had been attributed to one writer was frequently distributed among several. And the results were even more unsettling when the investigation passed from the Lower and Higher to Historical Criticism. The early narratives of Genesis were judged to be myth, the later to be legend, and even when real history was reached with Moses many of the details of the story were regarded as unhistorical. The same freedom of attitude was adopted with reference to the later history and in particular the Gospel story. Here at the very citadel of our religion the critic pressed home his scrutiny for the vulnerable points.

I pass on to the permanent results of criticism in our estimate of the Bible. It has in the first place given us a view of Scripture which corresponds more closely than the earlier theories with the actual phenomena of Scripture. Their tendency was to be at once too narrow and too wide; to concentrate the Divine revelation and inspiration in the written word, and at the same time to make claims for the individual parts in isolation which were not really justified. Owing to the idea that Scripture contained everywhere the immediate word of God to the soul, the theory of Scripture was unduly atomistic; and since experience did not show that all parts of Scripture did convey a blessing, the inevitable result was that large portions were either not read at all or, if read, yielded profit only at a few points. Even the prophets, in whose writings the Old Testament reaches its climax, were read largely in fragments. One of the chief results of our modern study has been that we have learnt to appreciate Scripture as a whole and to recognize the permanent value of much which in itself could hardly be said to convey any direct spiritual or moral lesson. The supreme achievement of our modern study has been that it has forced upon us the fact that God has revealed Himself through history and experience. To bring out the full significance of this would require a long discussion. I must indicate in the briefest way the positions which are implicit in it. It has shown us that the action of the Spirit is to be sought primarily in the history itself. The Bible contains the record of that Divine movement which, beginning in the dim antecedents of Israel's history, worked alike in the chosen people as a whole, and pre-eminently in elect individuals till it achieved its climax in the Person, the teaching and the Work of Christ, and the interpretation given to these by the New Testament writers. From this standpoint we can give a meaning and permanent significance to much in the Bible which it was difficult to claim for it from the older point of view. There is much which, when detached from the whole, has little or no value, but which may be indispensable for the appreciation of the whole. Much in the Old Testament, several things in the New, have to be judged on this principle. It is only on this principle that the permanent value of the Old Testament can be vindicated. No doubt, considerable sections would always hold their place for their inspiring eloquence, their lofty morality, their soaring spirituality, their fascinating romance. But it is not these qualities which would ensure them a place in the Canon of Scripture, in view of the fact that much of its teaching has been rendered obsolete by the Gospel. From this point of view we understand why it has pleased God that Scripture has included much which from the Christian standpoint is not simply obsolete but objectionable. It is because only so can the full import of the Spirit's action be rightly understood. The answer to many objections which have been supposed to discredit the Bible is to be found in a true understanding of what the Bible is. It is not primarily a manual either of theology or of ethics, but it is the record of God's gradual self-disclosure, of the Spirit's leavening of a material often too uncongenial. It was this too self-willed and too intractable medium which He had to subdue to His purpose, and the Old Testament records for us the wonderful story of His progressive mastery of His instrument. Only in fragmentary portions, as the author of the Epistle to the Hebrews has told us, was it possible for God to speak to His ancient people; it was only in a Son who was the radiance of His glory and the clear-cut impress of His essential being that He could fully translate Himself into human speech and express Himself in a human experience.

And this leads us to the further result that we have come to recognize the glorious variety of Scripture. We do not find that the Biblical writers always express themselves in accordance with the same scheme of doctrine, not even in the New Testament, still less in the Old. We can frame no satisfactory theology by an indiscriminate collection and arrangement of all the Biblical statements on each subject. The whole movement of revelation as an historical process must first be studied. Each writer must be placed in his context, and his theology as a whole so far as possible reproduced, and only when this has been done can the various types of theology be brought together and unified. Only in this way can we do justice to the rich and many-sided experience of the writers and the truths which have been conveyed through it. We can hardly over-emphasise the importance of the fact that while the Bible contains doctrines of the highest importance, it is primarily a book of experimental religion; and that the truths it enshrines did not come simply as direct communications of theological propositions, but were realized through doubts and misgivings, through wrestlings of the soul with God, through long and perplexed groping, or through some sudden and radiant flash of insight. And it is this human element which gives the Bible so much of its appeal to the human heart, and stamps it with such marks of authenticity. If we go expecting to find a body of doctrine formulated with scientific precision, or an accurate record of events such as a modern historian would give us, we may be disappointed. But we find something far better: we find life itself, the interaction of the Divine and the human in a great national history, and the experiemce of many an elect spirit. We may lose in abstract correctness, but we gain in warmth and interest. The teaching may not be so instantly available as if the Bible had been restricted to a series of theological and moral statements accurately expressed and duly co-ordinated into a system. But the difficulty in disengaging them from the history in which they are embedded is far more than balanced by the vital experimental quality conferred on them by the process through which they have come. Whatever be the conclusions of criticism the fact of the Bible remains; and it may truly be called a colossal fact.

HISTORY AS A CHANNEL OF REVELATION

IF we ask as to the record of Israel's religion contained in the Old Testament we may summarize certain of its main features as follows: There is, to begin with, a doctrine of God to which no other pre-Christian religion presents any parallel. He was of course realized as the living God, intensely personal, far removed from the Absolute of the speculative philosopher. So far indeed that at first He is presented to us in a very human way, limited by human imperfections, marred too often by a ruthless ferocity. But no goddess reigned by His side, so that the foul sexual licence in which kindred peoples found a congenial expression for their religion, was hateful in His sight. He was from the outset regarded as a righteous Deity, the vindicator of justice and the defender of the oppressed. For Israel He stood as the sole object of worship. He was a jealous God who would tolerate no rival. With the teaching of the great prophets the cruder features were refined away and the earlier limitations transcended. Although metaphysic was alien to the Hebrew mind, a conception of God was reached in which metaphysical as well as ethical elements had their place. The eternity, the infinity, the spirituality of God are implied, though they are conveyed in popular language, not asserted in the formulae of the philosopher. But the emphasis is placed on His moral qualities, His holiness, His righteousness, revealed now in inflexible judgement and now in forgiving grace, His loving-kindness and His pity. He is the Creator of the universe whose forces are all at His disposal; He is the controller of history who overrules for His purpose the plans and achievements of the mightiest empires. Through all apparent defeat and inexplicable delay He is moving with serene confidence and sure directness to His long predestined goal. He waits till His time is ripe, while His foes thwart His designs and mock His weakness. But when He strikes, He strikes once and needs to strike no more. They that hate Him lick the dust, His servants are exalted and His Kingdom is set up on earth in power.

And as the conception of God was deepened and purified,

morality and religion also gained in elevation, in inwardness, and in purity. The character of God necessarily reacted on the human ideal, as the one was moralized so inevitably was the other. By many a stern lesson the people were taught that He who was of purer eyes than to look upon iniquity could endure it least of all in His own chosen people. The mass of the nation no doubt fell far below the ideal presented to them by their prophets and lawgivers; yet even they were conscious that a special standard was set before them, a feeling expressed in such a phrase as 'such things ought not to be done in Israel', or the condemnation on those who 'had wrought folly in Israel'. And it is the ideal rather than the often squalid reality that for our purpose it is important to notice. Justice in the law courts, integrity in commercial relationships, equity as between employer and employed, generosity in the treatment of the defenceless, the widow, the orphan, and the resident alien, humanity toward slaves, the repression of slander and falsehood, temperance, chastity, prudence, readiness to forgive injuries and to repay evil with good, these and other virtues were clearly taught the Israelite by precept and example. Not in the Decalogue with its too negative morality and its regard for rights which must not be invaded, but in some of the classical utterances of the prophets, now and again in the Psalms or in the Book of Proverbs, especially in such a great passage as Job's oath of self-vindication, we should seek for the loftiest expression of Old Testament ethics. Nor were the writers so absorbed in details that they could not rise to the expression of great principles. It is a Hebrew prophet who asks the question: 'What doth Yahweh require of thee but to do justly, to love mercy, and to walk humbly with thy God?' It is a Hebrew lawgiver to whom we owe the great precept, 'Thou shalt love thy neighbour as thyself'.

And in religion as well as ethics a very lofty level was attained. At first religion was primarily a relationship between God and the nation, involving mutual obligations both of a religious and of a moral kind, on which it is unnecessary to dwell. But with Jeremiah the individual came to his own, and although the sense of the bond between Yahweh and Israel remained unimpaired, the consciousness that the individual might have his own relationship to God became more and more widely diffused, and found many an expression in the later literature. To walk with God in humility and in confidence; to be assured of His goodness and His love, though the dark experiences of life seemed to mock such a trust; to obey His law, not with punctilious and painful exactness but with alacrity and joy; to make the moral ideal which was the expression of His will an integral part of the personality; to find in unbroken fellowship with Him life's perfect bliss; to mourn over sin with a passionate penitence; to long for cleansing and purity with an unquenchable desire; all this and more religion meant to the Old Testament saint.

Yet with all the great qualities which we find in the Old Testament, we must not forget its limitations. We ought not of course to lay any undue stress on the lower elements in the book, whether theologically crude or morally repellent, at least where these had been left behind. They are valuable as landmarks on Israel's upward way. Yet we must beware of the opposite danger, that of taking the Old Testament at its best, in those rare and outstanding passages where it approximates to Christianity, as if they gave us a just measure of its true character. And judging it with these cautions in our mind we cannot be blind to its limitations. It contains, especially in its later sections, a highly developed and clearly expressed monotheism. Yet it largely neutralized its own achievement by its special appropriation of God. The nations belonged to Yahweh no doubt, but Yahweh belonged to Israel; an attitude which found expression sometimes in the thought that while the Gentiles were ultimately to be brought into the Kingdom of God, they were yet to be subservient to Israel, sometimes in lurid and exultant anticipations of the fiery judgement which was to come upon them. Again, one may rightly recognize a real advance in the centralization of the cultus at Jerusalem. The suppression of the high places eliminated many abuses at one stroke, and secured a far more effective supervision. Yet the limitation to locality was a mark of the imperfection of the religion. It was transcended when the words were uttered 'Neither in this mountain nor yet in Jerusalem shall men worship the Father.' Further, the physical element was over-emphasized. Physical victims offered on material altars in a material structure by priests whose tenure of office was conferred by physical descent, these were the media through which the worshippers drew near to God and sought to cleanse their conscience from the guilt of sin. Similarly the ancient system of taboo had survived in the laws of clean and unclean, into which it is true some spiritual meaning might be put, but which were essentially irrational none the less. Food taboos, such as are familiar among savage peoples, are present in the legislation in considerable numbers and reduced to system. Physical states which were inevitable or accidental and to which no ethical quality attached were pronounced unclean and an elaborate ritual was enjoined for their purification. The ideal of religion, especially in Judaism, was legalistic, the relation between God and man was conceived as a matter of merit to be achieved by a man's own acts. Legalism led naturally to an unhealthy casuistry and often to a self-righteous temper. Nor had the Old Testament any assured doctrine of immortality in the higher sense of the term. The persistence of the human spirit after death was generally accepted, but we could hardly dignify this flickering consciousness, which just held on to existence, with the name of 'life' in any worthy sense of the term. We can trace in the Old Testament the beginning of a higher belief. Sometimes this took the form of a doctrine of resurrection, the body being recalled from the grave and the shade from Sheol, and the reunited personality living on earth in the Messianic period. Sometimes, however, the conviction is expressed that death itself cannot destroy the fellowship of the saint with his God but that the disembodied spirit will within the veil enjoy a blessed immortality in His presence. But these loftier flights of faith are rare indeed; in the main we must say that the Old Testament stands at the lower level. It was, therefore, natural that the evidence of God's favour should be sought especially in material prosperity and length of days, and virtue be commended as the passport to their attainment. The truth expressed in Bacon's well-known aphorism that prosperity is the beatitude of the Old Testament and adversity the beatitude of the New very well expresses one of the limitations of the earlier literature.

But it may be said, Has the Old Testament not been left behind? Has it any significance for ourselves today? Our very conception of it as the history of a long development in which stage after stage was outgrown reminds us that even the highest stage it reached was outgrown at last. The Gospel came and superseded all that had gone before. To this question I shall return, but I cannot ignore the fact that the movement of which I have been speaking did not come to its close with the Old Testament. The supreme type of religion is the Gospel, and it is revealed to us not in the Old Testament but in the New.

We cannot of course forget that the preparation for Christianity was many-sided. The Gospel came, as was fitting, in the fullness of time, when many lines of progress converged to create the best conditions for the spread of the new religion. Many states and civilizations had been unified in the Roman Empire. The diffusion of Greek gave to the missionaries of the Cross a language in which they could preach their faith to the most varied races, and to its theologians a flexible and subtle terminology exquisitely adapted to express the finest shades of meaning. The old religions had largely lost their hold, there was a breakdown of morality on a large scale. And this bankruptcy of the old world in faith and conduct prepared men to turn with eagerness to a Gospel which offered power to the broken will and healing to the broken heart. Yet it is not on these things that our mind chiefly dwells when we speak of the preparation for Christianity, but rather on the history of the religion of Israel. Here rather than in the Imperial system which furnished the conditions in which the Gospel might win its peaceful triumphs, or the creation by Greece of the moulds into which its thought might be cast, or even in the aching heart that longed for nothing so much as peace, we find the most important factor in the preparation for the new religion. Jesus knew Himself to be the final revelation of God, since He was the Son of God, standing in a relationship to Him unshared by angel or man. Yet, while He stood in lonely greatness above Moses and the Prophets, and set the Law aside without hesitation, He asserted His continuity with the old order, which He superseded by fulfilling it. We can as little deny His affinity to the Old Testament as we can deny His matchless originality.

And the religion which Jesus came to establish was the final revelation of God. It was a revelation given through teaching, but even more through act. Its message was clothed in language of wholly new charm and beauty. Its doctrine of God was more tender and gracious and yet free from all touch of weakness or sentimentalism. Its ethical ideal was more searching and more inward, loftier in its demand, yet filled with a new sweetness and inspired by a warmer, humaner spirit. A new worth was attributed to the individual, even the meanest was of untold value to God. But greater still than the revelation in utterance was the revelation in character and action. The unearthly purity of Christ's life, the freedom from all self-seeking, the radiant certainty of God, the love which shrank from no sacrifice that it might redeem from sin, brought home to men an intimate realization of the character of God with which no earlier revelation can be even remotely compared. And while in the life and death of Jesus the revelation of God attained its climax, He also revealed for the first time the human ideal. In His perfect character there were blended all the virtues and graces in exquisite proportion and mutual adjustment, and yet not as a mere disconnected series but fused into a perfect unity by the personality to which they belonged. Thus we may say that the Person of Jesus, His teaching and His character, His life and His death, constituted the supreme revelation of God. Here, as before, that revelation comes as a process in history, a process by which God unveiled to us His nature and His love till we were able to bear the splendour and estimate the worth of His loftiest self-manifestation. And as the Old Testament contains the story of the earlier stages in this process, so the Gospels embody the story of God's last and greatest utterance.

II—BIBLICAL
THE TEACHING OF JEREMIAH

IT was not the manner of Hebrew writers to argue for the existence of God, or elaborately to define Him. They had little concern with speculative problems, and even the godless scorners who said 'There is no God' were guilty not of theoretical but of practical atheism. The task of their prophets and lawgivers was not to give them a firmer assurance of the reality of the God they worshipped, but to insist that the deities they set by His side were unrealities, and to purify their worship from materialistic and immoral elements. To this Jeremiah forms no exception. His own sense of God was so immediate and convincing, his consciousness of intimate fellowship so clear, that he would have been under even less temptation to doubt His existence than those who had derived their belief only from unquestioned tradition. The urgent questions were rather those suggested by the heathen tendencies of his countrymen, the recognition of Canaanite and foreign deities, the assimilation of Yahweh to them, the disbelief in His moral government. Whether we should speak of Jeremiah as a speculative monotheist may be debated. But practically his position was indistinguishable from monotheism. The gods of the heathen are no gods, they are vanities. Yahweh fills heaven and earth, none can elude His vigilance. He is the God of nature, who has set the sand as a bound of the sea; its mutinous waves may toss and roar, but their chafing at His curb is all in vain. He gives the rains in their season and harvest at the appointed time. He is the God of history; all nations, even the mightiest, are at His disposal and the instruments of His will. His character is to be inferred rather from His government of the world and His attitude to the conduct of His people than from the definite statements made by the prophet, though these are not wholly wanting. A characteristic utterance is 'I am Yahweh, which exercise lovingkindness, judgement, and righteousness in the earth: for in these things I delight'. With all the assertions of His sternness toward sin there is constant reference to His goodness, grace, and readiness to forgive. These and other qualities, however, will be more fully brought before us in the sequel.

When Jeremiah first appeared before his countrymen as the spokesman of Yahweh, he tenderly recalled the happy relations between Israel and her God in the days of the nation's youth. Like Hosea, from whom he has derived the symbol of marriage to express these relations, he looked back to the nomad period as Israel's best and happiest age. Even after the long centuries of unfaithfulness, Yahweh remembers in her favour the love she showed Him as a youthful bride when He had rescued her from Egypt, the loyalty with which she followed Him through the uncultivated desert. And her love was met by an answering love; she was sacred to Him as the first-fruits, which none might touch on pain of His vengeance. He led her through all the perils of the pathless uninhabited wilderness, and brought her into the fruitful land of Canaan. And then, as if He had given her just cause of displeasure, she turned away and went in pursuit of false gods, defiled His land and made it an abomination. Like a refractory ox she snapped yoke and thongs and renounced the service of her master. Forgetful of all His goodness she made light of her marriage vows, sinning with her many lovers on every lofty hill and under every leafy tree. It was no fault of His, who had planted her as a choice vine, that she had become a foreign vine. The fault was all her own. Yielding to the perilous fascination of the agricultural life she had gone after the Baalim, the givers of fertility as she fondly imagined. How madly she had acted! She had left the unfailing fountain of living waters and with much cost and toil hewed out cisterns in the rock, thinking thus the better to slake her feverish thirst with their foul and stagnant water which too often leaked away, leaving but a filthy sediment. As if the hot lustfulness and wild tumultuous excitement of Baal worship, the delirious raptures of a sensual religion, could bring her contentment and rest! Let East and West be ransacked for any parallel to her conduct and none would be found. For no other nation ever changed its gods, though they were but nonentities. But Israel has changed her God, who is her glory, for that which cannot profit.

This had been the sad history of the northern tribes as well as of Judah. And when the Northern Kingdom had disappointed Yahweh's expectation of reform, He put her away and gave her a bill of divorcement. Judah might have taken warning by her sister's exile, but she plunged even more deeply into sin. The story of the girdle ruined by Euphrates water was apparently intended to symbolize the religious and moral corruption of Israel by Assyrian and Babylonian influences. In the reign of Manasseh foreign cults had become more and more prominent. 'They did worse than their fathers', such is the prophet's verdict on the later apostasy of his people. The sun and moon and all the host of heaven were zealously worshipped, and the women were especially earnest in the cult of the Queen of Heaven. The hideous custom of child-sacrifice was practised in the Valley of Hinnom. It would seem that the people intended these gruesome offerings of their children for Yahweh, but He repudiates with horror all responsibility for this misapprehension.

Jeremiah had probably been familiar in early life with the popular worship of the country districts in the time of Manasseh and Amon, and we have no reason to suppose that matters had altered much when he received his call. The reformation did not take place till five years later, and his earliest prophecies permit us to reconstruct in some detail the religious conditions with which he was confronted at the opening of his ministry. The justice of the prophet's indictment would apparently not have been granted by the people. They indignantly repudiated the charge that they had gone after the Baalim. In reply he points to their 'way in the valley' by which he intends the sacrifice of children in the Valley of Hinnom; but they would have explained this as an example of their ardour in the service of Yahweh. To Jeremiah such a protestation counted for nothing. It seemed to him only a mark of Judah's deep insincerity. What mattered the mere name of the deity when the rites by which he was honoured were heathenish? And so he complains of the blandishments she lavishes on Yahweh, 'Hast thou not but just now cried unto me, My father, thou art the friend of my youth?' Yet all the while she is saying 'My father' or 'My mother' to stock and stone. The host of heaven, and especially the Queen of Heaven, are still assiduously worshipped. Judah is like a young she-camel at mating time, stung by passion, restlessly crossing and recrossing her tracks in her desire, uncontrollable with her insatiable lust. Like a shameless wanton she races after her lovers till her shoes fall from her feet and her throat is parched by thirst. She professes her inability to reform, for all self-control is lost; she loves the strange gods and after them she will go. Yet in the time of trouble it is from her own God that she claims deliverance, and, protesting her innocence, expostulates with Yahweh when calamity overtakes her, or reassures herself with the fond belief that His wrath will soon pass away; for she has learnt nothing from former chastisement.

But Yahweh views her conduct in a very different light. He sternly repels her deceitful endearments, and gives her unfaithfulness its dishonourable name. He answers her brazen assertion of her innocence with the threat that He will punish her for making it. How gladly, indeed, He would have dealt with her otherwise! He would have treated her as a son, waiving her inability as a daughter to inherit, and given her the goodliest heritage of the nations. But how can she expect Him to take her back? If a woman's first husband cannot receive her back after she has been divorced from him and united in legitimate marriage to another man, how can Yahweh receive her, who while still legally bound to Him has yet wronged Him by her sinful relations with many lovers? Her transgressions have been unpardonable, her guilt so ingrained that she cannot cleanse it away. Yet what would seem impossible to man is possible to God. Utterly defiled, irretrievably wicked as she seems to be, there is still an opportunity of repentance and amendment. On the bare heights, the scene of unnumbered sins, the prophet hears in imagination the brokenhearted wailing of his people in penitence for their unfaithfulness. And at once the inarticulate confession is met by Yahweh's gracious invitation to them to return, by His gracious promise that He will heal their apostasy. Then the people, who otherwise had not dared to address Him against whom they had transgressed so deeply, respond with the cry, 'We come to Thee, for Thou art our God', and with the confession that the sensuous orgies of their worship had brought them no real satisfaction. In Yahweh alone is salvation; the Baalim had robbed them not of animal victims alone, but of their sons and daughters. They would lie down overwhelmed by shame and confusion for their sin. Then Yahweh sets forth the conditions on which she may return to Him and judgement be averted.

Alas! it was only in imagination that the prophet heard his people weeping for their sins. They seemed deaf to his appeals. He still continues to preach amendment, but in vain. He reiterates his charges of idolatry. But now he enters more closely into other forms of sin. His observation has led him to a pessimistic verdict. Rich and poor, teacher and taught, are all alike. It is a foolish, sottish people, wise to do evil, but with no knowledge to do good. One might ransack Jerusalem and fail to find a single individual who acts justly or seeks faithfulness. Men wax rich by deceit, and grow sleek by oppression, they wrest justice from the fatherless and the needy. All are given to covetousness and false dealing. Jerusalem keeps her wickedness fresh as a cistern keeps its water cool. Violence and spoil, sickness and wounds are to be found in her. The sanctities of the home are set at naught by widespread immorality. The great men who know God's will are defiant and refractory, and have not the excuse of ignorance which may be urged for the poor. The religious leaders, the priests and prophets, have entered into an unholy conspiracy, and the people love to be misguided by them. They give medical attention to the wound of the people, but content themselves with a superficial treatment of the symptoms instead of the drastic surgery which its gravity demands. Thus the prophet's prolonged assaying of his people has brought him to the melancholy conviction that there is no pure metal in them. For such a people, incredulous though it be of calamity, nothing remains except national destruction. No frankincense from Sheba, no calamus from a distant country, will be of avail to avert it; burnt offerings and sacrifices will prove unacceptable. The foe from the north comes on to inflict Yahweh's vengeance. The people are inflammable wood, and the prophetic word in Jeremiah's lips is the fire which will kindle them.

The Deuteronomic reformation made an end of idolatry and of the heathenish rites which had invaded the worship of Yahweh. The suppression of the local sanctuaries and the concentration of the cultus at the Temple did much to purify religion. We are not in a position to follow the course of the prophet's ministry in the later part of Josiah's reign, so we do not know how he would have estimated the character of the people during that period. But we have reason to believe that he would soon perceive that the wound of the people had again been too lightly healed. When we come to Jehoiakim's reign we have ample evidence. It is not clear indeed to what extent idolatry had returned or the worship of the local sanctuaries been restored. The great address delivered at the Temple at the beginning of the reign charges the people with sacrificing to the Baal and walking after other gods, and the description of the worship offered to the Queen of Heaven is at present incorporated in the report of that address, though it may not have originally been included in it. In the same address we find reference to the abominations which have defiled the Temple, and the sacrifice of children in the Valley of Hinnom. But we have to allow for the possibility that these allusions were rather to the state of things in the pre-reformation period, and further that they may be due in some measure to later interpolation. For the altercation which took place in Egypt between Jeremiah and the devotees of the Queen of Heaven strongly favours the view that there had been no revival of her cult in Judah, since they trace their misfortunes, culminating in their present evil case, to its cessation. We need not, on the other hand, deny that a good deal of idolatry probably went on, or that worship may have been revived at many of the high places. This would, we may presume, be of an unofficial character, there would be no formal repeal of Josiah's reforms or any re-establishment of cults he had suppressed. And this applies to the subsequent reigns, during which, as we learn from Ezekiel, sun worship, animal worship, and the wailing of women for Tammuz were practised, unless here again we ought to regard the description as referring to what had gone on at an earlier time.

The attack on other forms of sin naturally assumes greater prominence in the post-reformation period, but there is little to add to what has been already said. Theft, murder, adultery, perjury, oppression of the defenceless, the maladministration of justice, constitute along with idolatry, the black catalogue of crimes and vices, which unless they cease from them will bring on the Temple the fate of Shiloh, and on the Jews an exile like that of Ephraim. Elsewhere the prophet complains bitterly of the deceit and treachery which have undermined all mutual confidence, and poisoned all social intercourse. While their sin assumed many forms, fundamentally it was the refusal to hearken to God's commands given through His prophets. He had been unwearied in sending them to recall His erring people to the ancient paths, that in them they might find rest for their souls. But as Yahweh's child, Israel had repaid His love with ungrateful disobedience, as His wife she had broken her marriage vows. It was in the wrong relation to God that the root of all the mischief was to be found.

No lavish ceremonial or costly sacrifices, no loyalty to the Temple could commend to His favour a people stained with such sins. So valueless in His eyes are their sacrifices that He tells them to take the burnt-offerings, reserved for Himself alone, and eat these as well as those sacrifices of which the worshippers partook; they were nothing but ordinary flesh robbed of all the sanctity which their consecration on the altar would otherwise have conferred.

But the most characteristic element in Jeremiah's doctrine of sin has not yet been mentioned, or he would not have made any essential advance on the prophets who preceded him. Gifted beyond all others with psychological insight and a keenness of introspection, he is not content with a merely empirical description of the manifestations which sin assumes. With delicate analytic skill he takes them back to their cause, which he finds in the evil heart of man, defiant of God's control, obstinate in taking its own course. Not, indeed, that this evil heart was an original factor in human nature. This might seem to be suggested by his famous question: 'Can the Ethiopian change his skin, or the leopard his spots?' For we might infer that he held evil to be as integral a part of man's nature as the colour of an Ethiopian's skin or the spots in a leopard's hide, and therefore as ineffaceable. But when he continues, 'then may ye also do good that are accustomed to do evil', we see that the inference would be mistaken. Their moral inability was due not to any radical quality of nature, but to long-protracted habit. If the stork in the heaven knows her appointed times, if the turtle and the swift and the swallow observe the time of their coming, then surely man must have an instinct within him to guide him to God and to duty as unerring as that which prompts at the right season the migration of the birds. But, unlike them, he has disobeyed the instinct so that his heart has become blunted in its delicate susceptibilities to right and wrong, and can never, till it has been circumcised, recover its fine and true moral and religious sensitiveness. The heart of man, even in his own case, he knows to be 'deceitful above all things and desperately sick', so intricate in its tortuous windings that God alone can search and know the man as he is in his inmost self. And this preoccupation with the heart as the source of conduct, this change in the centre of gravity from the outward to the inward, forced him into an individualism in his conception of sin corresponding to that which we find in his portrayal of the moral and spiritual ideal in his doctrine of the New Covenant. So he does not content himself with an indictment against society and the State. He singles out the individuals of whom society is composed, and pronounces all without exception unclean. If there were but one righteous man in Jerusalem God would pardon the city. Hence he addresses himself not simply to the nation as a whole, but he bids each individual turn from his evil way.

From his pessimistic estimate of his people there followed an equally pessimistic forecast of the future. Not, indeed, that he allowed his efforts for their regeneration to be paralysed by the gloominess of his outlook. Their case was in truth desperate, but he put a desperate energy into his pleadings with them. Their light-hearted optimism made him despair of influencing them. Entrenched in the dogma that Zion was impregnable, complacently assured of their good standing with their God, they treated his warnings as the dreams of a fanatic whom the event had often discredited. And in their refusal to believe such blasphemy as that the Temple would share the fate of Shiloh, that Jerusalem would be destroyed and the nation hurled into exile, they had the support of the official representatives of religion.

But though Jeremiah strove with such earnestness to wake his people from a slumber that could end only in death, in his heart of hearts he had all but abandoned hope. The very appearance of a true prophet had always been a presage of disaster, a sure indication that Yahweh was meditating some terrible judgement on His people. This judgement might be averted by timely repentance, but in the temper of Judah Jeremiah detected no sense of need, no consciousness of realities. From the outset his message had been primarily one of breaking down and plucking up, and he never faltered in his conviction that God would speak His judgements against His people by the foe out of the north. The enemy sweeps on swift as a whirlwind, multitudinous and invincible, cruel and pitiless; the inhabitants flee for refuge into the fortified cities while invaders ravage the land, devouring their corn and fruit, their flocks and herds. But even in the cities they are not safe, for Jerusalem itself will not withstand the besiegers. Pestilence, famine, and sword will do their work and the remnant will go into exile. The city will become a heap of ruins, a haunt of jackals. The dead will lie unburied on the ground with none to bewail them. The foe will take the bulk of the population in great masses as fish are captured in a net, and then they will hunt out those that are left one by one from every chink and cranny of the hills and rocks where they have taken refuge. Thus the land will be completely denuded of its inhabitants. The sound of merriment will be hushed, the voice of the bridegroom and bride, a deathly stillness will brood over the land unbroken by the sound of the mill, nor will the darkness of night be relieved by the light of the cottage lamp. It is as though chaos had come back: the heavens are shrouded in blackness, no human form meets the eye of the prophet as it ranges over the landscape nor any bird in the sky, the fertile country has become desert, the cities are beaten down. And those who escape with their lives and are taken into exile will envy the dead, so wretched will be their lot, as they are tossed to and fro among the nations, dashed against each other without pity, and pursued by the sword till they are consumed. Moreover, the fall of Judah will involve that of the surrounding peoples, who also will be made to drink the wine from the goblet of God's anger.

But punishment is not God's last word to Judah. True, His anger will not be spent so soon as the optimists imagine, for seventy years must go by before the Babylonian empire falls. But at last the day of deliverance will dawn. In his early ministry Jeremiah had anticipated the return of the northern tribes and their joyous life in the land of their fathers. And for the exiles of Judah who have been taken to Babylon he expresses a similar hope. They must meanwhile make themselves at home in their new country and wait God's good time. But on these exiles, though not on those in Egypt, Yahweh has set His eyes for good and not for evil, and at last He will restore them to their own land. Israel and Judah will be reunited and live in peace and prosperity under native rulers. And this manifestation of God's might and favour will so far surpass the deliverance from Egypt that they will cease to say 'As Yahweh liveth, which brought up the children of Israel out of the land of Egypt' and will say 'As Yahweh liveth, which brought up and which led the seed of the house of Israel out of the north country, and from all the countries whither He had driven them'. And over this people thus happily reunited there will reign the Messianic king. He is described as a righteous Shoot. He is of David's race and will fulfil the ideal of a just and wise monarch, who keeps his people in security and peace. He will bear the name

'Yahweh is our righteousness' and realize, as Zedekiah did not, the ideal implied in the name. It is noteworthy that in Jeremiah's doctrine of the Messiah there is, as we should anticipate, a welcome absence of those unhallowed dreams of far-extended empire, of the heathen annihilated or crushed into abject slavery, such as stain so many Messianic forecasts in the canonical and post-canonical literature of Judaism.

Such then, is his political ideal. And his religious and ethical ideal corresponds to it. Alike for nation and individual he deprecates all trust in the arm of flesh. In a beautiful passage he draws a contrast between the man who trusts in man and makes flesh his arm and whose heart departs from Yahweh, and the man whose trust is reposed in Him. And similarly he would have his people abandon the vain hope of help from foreign powers and rely on the living God alone. To Him alone glory belongs, and man must stand before Him in humility and awe. None should glory in his own wisdom, his might or his wealth, but only in his understanding and knowledge of Yahweh, that it is He who executes kindness, judgement, and righteousness in the earth. It goes without saying that the prophet took for granted in the happy future which he anticipated for the people a complete abandonment of all those vices and crimes which he had had such constant occasion to rebuke in his own generation.

But his supreme contribution to religion still remains to be mentioned. It corresponds in its inwardness to his conception of sin. This is his doctrine of the New Covenant. It stands contrasted with the Old Covenant, that made by Yahweh with Israel at the Exodus, inscribed with God's finger on the Tables of the Law, or written in a book. That covenant Israel had broken, and Yahweh had cancelled it before all the world by the destruction of the Temple and the exile of the nation. But He had annulled it, not because the sin of Israel had so wearied Him that His patience was exhausted, but because Israel had proved unequal to the demand it made. An external law had proved a failure, man's evil heart had paralysed its power to control the conduct of nation or individual. A new method had accordingly to be tried, which should deal radically with the seat of the evil. Since it was the stubbornness of the heart, its obstinate defiance of God's commandments, which had made the Old Covenant so ineffective, He would inaugurate a New Covenant and secure its success by capturing

THE TEACHING OF JEREMIAH

the stronghold which had so long maintained rebellion against Him, the heart which is the citadel of man's being. He would put His laws in men's inward parts and write them on their heart. This must be read in the light of what is said elsewhere, which implies a transformation of the heart. It is not the writing of Divine commands on a heart which is still rebellious that is intended. The heart is itself renewed, so that there is no conflict between the Divine injunction and the nature which is summoned to fulfil it. It is a circumcised heart, a heart from which the old moral and religious insensibility has been removed. The law of God and the heart of man no longer stand opposed to each other as external and internal. Man does God's will naturally and spontaneously because it is his own will, it has become an integral part of his personality, the law of his nature. In other words, it is not merely an intuitive knowledge of God's will that is intended. This would be secured by the writing of the law on the unregenerate heart, but the problem of obedience would be as far as ever from solution. Only when the heart itself had been renewed, when its refractory hostility to God's behests had been subdued, would not only the knowledge of His will but the conformity to it be achieved.

Yet we must not undervalue the advance in the matter of knowledge which the New Covenant marked over the Old. A Code of Laws designed for large masses of people is inevitably of a generalizing character, it is lacking in flexibility and delicate adjustment to individual conditions. To correct this defect of rough approximation the legislator might look to a developed system of casuistry constructed with the aim of registering and legislating for all possible cases. But such an aim is quite unattainable in view of the variety and complexity of the characters and conditions themselves, and still more of the intricate situations to which their interaction gives rise. Conduct would become for the expert a matter of painfully regulated conformity with this code, from which all the bloom and aroma of unconsciousness and spontaneity would have departed. The ordinary man, on the other hand, would have to content himself with such vague extensions and applications of the law as his personal circumstances and temperament or the lessons of experience might suggest. What is really required is the power of instinctive and instantaneous self-adjustment to every situation as it arises, the knowledge of the exact response that should be made to the stimulus which each brings with it. Such an ideal it is the purpose of the New Covenant to attain. Thus what the Law could not do, in virtue of its general and external character, God would accomplish under the New Covenant, by giving men a heart to know Him (24[7]) and then placing within this renewed heart His law as the spring of all action.

It is clear that if God gives to each a heart to know Him, no need would any longer exist for one to exhort another to acquaint himself with God. All would know Him from the least to the greatest. The relation of God to the individual would be immediate and direct, independent of the State or official order of religious teachers. It would nevertheless be a mistake to interpret Jeremiah as the prophet of an atomistic individualism. An individualist he was, and that in full measure. But the New Covenant itself is made with the nation. The religion remains the religion of Israel, a national religion. God and Israel are still the contracting parties to the New Covenant as to the Old. But the individualism which characterized the New made the religion national in a sense unattainable under the Old. For when the religion rested on external guarantees and was expressed in external institutions, while its laws were imposed by an external authority, when moreover the people was contemplated as a unit, without reference to the individuals of whom it was composed, then it was national, but in a general and superficial sense. Only when every individual in the mass is renewed in heart and his will brought into harmony with the Divine will, can the nation itself be truly called religious. Through its individualism the religion first became national in the full sense of the term.

What, then, of the dark apostasy which through their long history in Canaan had stained the history alike of Judah and Israel? What of the sins which had been committed by those who thus experienced this renewal of heart and implanting of the Divine Law? A complete amnesty is promised, God will pardon their iniquities and remember them no more. Only with such forgiveness and forgetfulness could happy relations between them be restored. Nothing is said in the passage of the conditions which made pardon and oblivion possible. It is of course assumed that the people have turned to God in penitence for their rebellion and with fervent determination to obey His will. But Jeremiah, like the Old Testament writers generally, while he recognizes that punishment is often inflicted on sin, seems to feel no difficulty in the Divine forgiveness of sin on the sole condition of repentance.

We cannot easily overestimate the significance of Jeremiah's doctrine of the New Covenant. It is the supreme achievement of Israel's religion, and its author was the loftiest religious genius who adorned the line of the prophets. For whereas other prophets did much to interpret religion and enforce its demands, he transformed the very conception of religion itself. Hitherto religion had been the concern of the nation with its God, the individual had no independent standing before the Deity. Not indeed, that what we call personal religion was unknown, but that the stress lay on the national relationship, and the individual had no claim on his God apart from his connexion with his people. Jeremiah shifts the emphasis from the nation to the individual. The essence of religion he discovers in a personal relation to a personal God, where in fact it lies. Each knows God for himself, in the heart of each God places His law. His doctrine was thus an anticipation of the Gospel in that it asserted the worth of the individual to God and the personal character of religion, in its assurance of forgiveness, its transcendence of legalism, and the inwardness of its ethic. It might seem as if even Jeremiah failed to rise above the nationalism from which the religion of Israel never succeeded in escaping, since he still regards the covenant as made with Israel and Judah. But here it is necessary to distinguish between kernal and husk. It is true that his doctrine as stated in this passage is justly charged with this limitation. Elsewhere indeed he anticipates a conversion of the heathen (12^{15-16}, 16^{19-20}). This anticipation, however, perhaps scarcely coincides with universalism in the full sense of the term. But it could hardly be expected that even Jeremiah should take the step from nationalism into universalism, for which he would have felt no warrant, even if the thought had dawned upon him, and for which in fact the time had not come. Yet while formally religion remained national in his doctrine, essentially the national restrictions were surmounted. For religion, as he conceived it, was really independent of race and country. It needed no external embodiment, even the ark had ceased to possess any spiritual value. Religion, as he defined it, was not fitly confined to a single people: it was not a relationship between God and the Israelite, but between God and man. The universalism of Christianity was logically implicit in it.

The verses in which the doctrine is enshrined are not isolated in Jeremiah's teaching. They are the outcome of no transient flash of insight, which lit up for him spiritual depths he had never before explored. They are the ripe fruit of long experience, of deep meditation on the ultimate realities of the spiritaul life. It was not given to him that he should clothe his thoughts in their most radiant expression. But if to the author of the seventy-third Psalm it was granted to utter once for all the blessedness of the soul to which naught in heaven or earth seems precious save fellowship with the living God, he strikes in that utterance a note made possible by Jeremiah. The experience was verified by the Psalmist; it had been discovered by Jeremiah. He was the first to break through the crust of nationalism to the glowing centre of religion. And he who first proclaimed the truth that religion is in its essence the communion of the individual with God, must for ever rank as one of the world's supreme discoverers in the greatest of all realms.

THE TEACHING OF THE EPISTLE TO THE HEBREWS

THE subject of the Epistle is 'the world to come' (2^5) and it is developed by an elaborate contrast with this present world. The world to come does not bear its name because it has yet to come into being. It already exists, and has existed from eternity. It is regarded as still to come, because as yet it has not been realized in time. Our world is but its copy, created in time and destined in the imminent convulsion of heaven and earth to pass away. It is the earthly and material as contrasted with the heavenly and spiritual, the temporal and perishable as contrasted with the eternal and permanent. Two orders of things thus exist side by side, a higher and a lower, the pattern and the copy. But it is in the sphere of religion simply that the author works out the contrast. His starting-point is the lower order as instituted in the Law and its ritual. From the known he argues to the unknown. Moses had been commanded to make all things according to the pattern shown him in the mount (9^5). This pattern was the true, original tabernacle, which the Lord pitched, not man (8^2) and since it was exactly copied in the material order, its form and internal arrangements could be inferred from those of the earthly tabernacle. Yet in the very fact that it belonged to the heavenly order, it was implied that it was not made with hands, was no tangible (12^{18}) or material structure. Its home was in the realm of ideas, as they live in the mind of God. This is not to say that it was a mere abstraction, a thought which lacked all reality till it was embodied in a material form. That would almost invert the true relation. The material is not the real, but its insubstantial shadow. No material imitation can give the actual image of the spiritual. It has no permanence; as it came, so it will perish in time. The ideal tabernacle is the truly real, since it is the spiritual and eternal, unfettered by the limitations of space or time, its inherent energies unsapped by the decay which exhausts the vitality of all earthly things. The main thesis of the author is that Christianity is superior to Judaism and is the perfect religion, because it belongs to the heavenly order, while Judaism belongs to the earthly and is stamped with its ineffectiveness.

The whole argument we might almost say, falls under this contrast of material and spiritual, of temporal and eternal. It might seem inconsistent with this that the author places in the forefront of his discussion the superiority of the Son to the angels. Do not the angels then, belong to the spiritual and eternal order? It is true that they are the firstborn, enrolled in the city of God. Yet Jewish theology connected them closely with the material universe, so that each thing, even the most insignificant, had its angel. And the writer asserts that such tenure of personality as they may possess is so slight that God transforms them into impersonal natural forces (1^7). While the universe, with which they are inseparably connected, passes away, the Son's throne is for ever and ever. The law itself, which they gave (2^2) was ushered in with congenial exhibition of elemental phenomena (12^{18-21}) making the physical senses quail with intolerable fear. Its scene was a material mount, dissolving in flame, fenced from all access by physical bounds. Moses and Joshua were weak, mortal men, who at the best could give their followers an unquiet settlement in an earthly land, but could not lead them into the rest of God. And the whole religious apparatus of Judaism was of this physical character. Its priesthood was ever changing, for its priests were subject to death; its succession depended on physical descent, the qualifications or disqualifications for it were physical. It was subject to infirmity just because it was constituted by the law of a fleshen commandment. The tabernacle which it served was pitched by human hands and decked with a golden splendour, which made only the more glaring its spiritual indigence and moral inefficiency. Its sacrifices belonged wholly to the earthly order, the blood of animal victims could cleanse the flesh but not the conscience, the material sanctuary but not the things in the heavens; and thus the access it could give to God was a mere make-believe. The covenant thus dedicated and maintained by physical blood-sprinkling, since it could not take away sin, and thus could provide no real fellowship with God, failed as a religion and hence could have no permanence. Moving wholly in the realm of the sensuous it could effect no spiritual result.

But Christianity is that heavenly original of which Judaism is the flickering and insubstantial shadow. Its revealer is no perishable angel, who lives only that he may serve, or ceases to live that as impersonal force he may serve the better. He is the eternal Son, Creator of the universe and Lord of the world to come. Radiance of the Divine glory and expression of the Divine essence he was the perfect revelation of God. Of heavenly origin, he could lead his followers into God's heavenly rest. As priest of the order of Melchizedek, with no beginning of days or end of life, his priesthood was unbroken by death. Nor did it rest on physical succession, but on personal worth. He offered no brute beast as his sacrifice, no irrational unconscious victim. He, God's eternal Son, was himself the victim whom he offered, in loving sympathy for his brethren, in loyal obedience to the Father's will. The sacrifice of such a Person, offered in such a spirit, released the most potent spiritual energies. It opened a new and living way into the heavenly tabernacle, where he presented himself as priest and victim in one. He cleansed the heavenly sanctuary, removing the veil, which even in it separated the Holy Place from the Holiest of all, and hid the face of God. Hence, while the Law was impotent to purge guilt away and bade the worshipper stand back, the blood of Christ cleansed the conscience and bade men draw nigh. So in the New Covenant, which he instituted, real communion with God first became possible, and the hindrances to it on God's side and on man's were taken away. Thus Christianity proved itself to be the perfect religion, in that it perfectly satisfied the religious instinct for fellowship with God.

The two orders exist side by side and come into relation in the sphere of human life. Man himself belongs to both. He is partaker of flesh and blood, subject to infirmity and death; yet he is a son of the Father of spirits, and a brother of the eternal Son, who did not become his brother through the Incarnation, but became incarnate because he was already man's brother and recognized the claims of brotherhood. It is the competition of these antagonistic elements that creates the moral tragedy of man's career, and sets the speculative problem, which the author attempts to solve. As linked to the sensuous he is a victim of sin, as a son of God he seeks communion with his heavenly Father. But sin fills him with the consciousness of unfilial disobedience, which forbids this fellowship. A sensuous sacrifice cannot cleanse the conscience, it only aggravates the sense of sin by the constant reminder of what it is powerless to remove. It is thus man's misery that, poised between two worlds, he cannot heartily belong to either. If he is to achieve his destiny to be lord of the world to come, powers must stream forth from that world and redeem him. Even before the coming of Christ, gleams of the heavenly order burst through. But the light was shattered in separate rays and fitful flashes. The Law was a shadow cast into the world by the heavenly reality, but with none of the religious power of its original. After the long preparation in the religious history of Israel the crisis arrived. The Son moved with love for his brethren, and desirous of offering a sacrifice agreeable to the will of God, clothed himself in a human body and struck into the current of human life. He lived within the terms of this lower order, became lower than the angels who ruled it, and placed the veil of flesh between himself and the heavenly world. He accepted all the conditions of a truly human life, especially the moral discipline of temptation. Thus, Son though he was, he learnt through pain a human obedience, passing through the utmost strain of temptation, till he became perfect through suffering. For that he might help his brethren in their temptations, might be their leader and priestly representative before God, he must gain a sympathy which not love itself, but only experience, could teach him. And yet while he had to share man's experience of temptation it was necessary that sympathy should not be purchased at the cost of sin. Only the sinless conqueror of temptation could be the Captain of salvation, only the morally spotless victim could be an acceptable sacrifice to God. And this intensified the keenness of his trial, for with him it passed the point at which other wills, even the strongest, had snapped under the strain. When the last lesson had been learnt in victory over the tremendous recoil from all that the cross implied, he became the High Priest of man. His offering of himself on the cross was itself a high-priestly act, for though locally it took place on earth, where he could not be a priest, it really belonged in virtue of its character to the heavenly order, since earthly and heavenly are matters not of space and time but of intrinsic quality. In death he broke free from the lower order, rending the veil of flesh, and passing into the heavenly sanctuary he presented himself before God. Thus having borne the sins which stained men's conscience with the sense of guilt he opened a path by which his fellows might enter into the immediate presence of their Father. But here the actual clashes with the ideal. Christians while on earth cast their anchor into the heavenly city, and are bound fast to it by the bond of hope. They are strangers and pilgrims, seeking a city and their fatherland. All things are not yet made subject to man; those who are called have received the promise of the eternal inheritance, but still await its fulfilment. On the other hand, they have already come to the heavenly city, to God and the angels, to Jesus and the spirits of the righteous made perfect. This double point of view answers to the double position which the Christian holds, and the double life he leads, in eternity and in time. Actually he still lives within the lower order. But ideally he has already transcended it, and he confidently looks forward to the time when the actual shall be one with the ideal. Yet this is not the whole truth. He need not wait till death rends the fleshen veil. 'We which have believed do enter into rest.' Faith has the power to translate us into the heavenly sanctuary, we may at any moment draw nigh and enjoy unrestricted communion with God.

III—THEOLOGICAL
THE QUINTESSENCE OF PAULINISM[1]

WHEN we speak of Paulinism we imply, first that Paul had a theology, and secondly that this theology was so distinctive that we are justified in using a specific name for it. Both contentions are exposed to criticism. Some would deem it a grave injustice to describe Paul as a theologian. He was rather a prophet, or even a poet, who felt deeply and had a keen insight into religious experience but was careless of logical consistency and indifferent to the creation of a system. Now it is true that Paul was gifted with the mystic's vision, and that in moments of ecstasy his utterance glows with a lyrical rapture. But it is part of his greatness that his thought is set on fire by noble emotion, and that emotion is redeemed from vagueness and incoherence by thought. Indeed the belief that Paul was a seer but no thinker could hardly survive a careful study even of one of his more characteristic writings. But, it may be retorted, Paul was in a sense a thinker, the sense in which a debater must be a thinker. In other words he is master of the argumentative style, and shows great skill in marshalling objections to the position of his opponents. He is a pleader rather than a philosopher. For my own part I believe that this is a profound mistake. Paul was not a mere controversialist who took the arguments that might be convenient for disposing of one antagonist without reference to their consistency with those he had used against another. Behind his occasional utterances there lies a closely knit and carefully constructed system of thought. He moves in his attack with such speed and confidence because he is in possession of a standard to which he relates each new issue as it confronts him. No series of hastily extemporized defences could have produced the same impression of unity and consistency unless they had belonged to a system. But in saying this I desire to disengage the word 'system' from any unfortunate association. It would be a

[1] An elaboration of the lecture delivered in the John Rylands Library, 11th October 1916.

serious misapprehension were we to think of Paulinism as representing for its author a complete and exact reflection of the whole realm of religious reality. He was indeed so convinced of the truth of his Gospel that he did not shrink from hurling an anathema at any, though it might be an angel from heaven, who should dare to contradict it. But his certainty as to the truth of his central doctrine did not blind him to the imperfection of his knowledge, or quench the sense of mystery with which he confronted the ultimate realities. He was conscious that beyond all the regions which he had explored and charted there stretched an illimitable realm, the knowledge of which was not disclosed in time but was reserved for eternity. Here he could prophesy only in part, because he was aware that he knew only in part; and though he soared, free and daring, in the rare atmosphere of speculative thought, he veiled his face in the presence of the ultimate mysteries. 'O the depth of the riches both of the wisdom and the knowledge of God! how unsearchable are His judgements, and His ways past finding out.'

Paul, then, believed himself to be in possession of a system of interdependent facts and ideas, arranged in due proportion and controlled from a centre. His epistles do not present us with a number of detached and independent ideas, still less with fluid opinions, fluctuating in response to changing conditions. He who builds on the Pauline theology, be that foundation false or true, ample, or inadequate, is building on firm granite, not on sinking and shifting sand. But some will challenge our right to use the term 'Paulinism'. It is, of course, true, they would say, that Paul had a coherent, self-consistent, and true system of thought. But this was just the same body of revealed truth as is present everywhere, explicitly or implicitly, in the New Testament, or even in the whole of Scripture. The traditional attitude to the Bible is that it everywhere says substantially the same thing on matters of doctrine, and that differences of expression involve no material disagreement. Now it may be argued, and with some measure of success, that beneath the various types of theology we find in the New Testament there is a fundamental harmony. But the science of Biblical Theology has demonstrated that these various types exist. It is accordingly our duty to study and estimate each of them for itself before we try to work behind them to a more fundamental unity. There is no type more distinctive, there is none so fully worked out as Paulinism.

The term 'Paulinism' might, of course, be used to cover the whole range of Paul's teaching; but I am concerned specially with those elements in it which were Paul's peculiar contribution to the interpretation of the Gospel. That contribution had its source, I believe, in the experience through which Paul passed. But he owed much to other influences. These affected, however, the distinctive elements of his teaching much less than those which he shared with his fellow-Christians. On this part of the subject I will dwell briefly, since it is rather my purpose to disengage from Paul's teaching as a whole that which is most characteristically his own. Of the external influences which originated or fashioned his doctrines I think we should attribute more to Hebrew, Jewish, and Christian theology than to Gentile philosophy or religious mysteries. It was inevitable that he should be profoundly impressed by the Old Testament. Apart from it, indeed, his theology could not have come into existence. It is the basis on which it rests, it largely supplied the moulds in which it was cast, and the substance as well as the form of much in the teaching itself. He presupposes the Old Testament, and regards his own doctrine as in continuity with it. When he became a Christian, he did not abandon the religion of Israel, but he saw in the Gospel the fulfilment and expansion of it. Yet it is a mistake to over-emphasize the Old Testament factor in the origin or formulation of Paulinism. Indeed that theology in one of its leading features is, from the Old Testament standpoint, a startling paradox. The estimate of the Law in the Old Testament is strangely different from that given by Paul. The Law inspires the Old Testament saints with a passionate devotion, as we may see from the glowing panegyric in the latter part of the nineteenth psalm, or the prolix enthusiasm of the hundred and nineteenth psalm. The ideal of the righteous man is the student whose delight is in the law of the Lord and who meditates upon it day and night. It is the safeguard and guide of youth, the stay of manhood, the comfort of age. It commanded more than sober approval or quiet acceptance; it drew to itself a passionate loyalty, an enthusiastic love, which nerved martyrs to face the most exquisite torture for its sake. But how different it is with Paul, who had himself in his earlier days experienced the same fervour as his countrymen, and indeed surpassed them in his zeal for it! It is true that even as a Christian he admits the sanctity and righteousness of the Law and the excellence of its purpose.

He recognizes in his philosophy of history a divinely appointed function for it. But for him the Law is no fount of refreshment and joy, it is a yoke and a burden, from which the Christian rejoices to be set free. It brings with it not a blessing but a curse. It is the instrument of sin, from which indeed that fatal tyrant draws its strength. It breaks up the old life of innocence by creating the consciousness of sin; it stimulates antagonism by its prohibitions, which suggest the lines of opposition along which the rebellious flesh may express its hostility. It was interpolated between God's gracious promise and its glorious fulfilment, that by its harsh and servile discipline men might be educated for freedom. So foreign, indeed, is the attitude of Paul to that of the Old Testament and Judaism, that one can easily understand how some Jewish scholars feel it hard to admit that anyone who had known Judaism from the inside could ever have written the criticism of the Law, which we find in the Epistles to the Romans and the Galatians. I believe that this is not so difficult if the problem is approached from the right starting-point; but it emphasizes the revolutionary character of the Pauline doctrine. Similarly I regard it as a serious error to interpret Paul's conception of the flesh by that which we find in the Old Testament. In the latter case it stands for human nature as a whole, the weak and perishable creature in contrast to the mighty immortals. The contrast gains occasionally a moral significance, but this is wholly subordinate. In Paul, however, instead of a metaphysical we have an ethical contrast. The flesh is not the synonym for man in his creaturely infirmity, whose moral lapses are indulgently excused by God as simply what must be expected from a being so frail and evanescent. It stands for one side only of human nature, that is the lower. It is evil through and through. It is so irretrievably the slave and instrument of sin, it is entrenched in such deep and abiding hostility to God and His will, that no redemption or even improvement of it is possible, it must be put to death on the cross of Christ. To reduce Paul's doctrine to the Old Testament level is to miss its tragic intensity and eviscerate it of its bitter moral significance.

If from the Old Testament we turn to the contemporary Judaism, there also we are constrained to admit a measure of influence on the apostle's thought. He had been a Pharisee, trained by Gamaliel. Naturally he did not break completely with the past when he became a Christian. He brought over current Jewish ideas and modes of argument. His Rabbinical interpretation of Scripture has been long familiar, but it is only within recent years that a fuller acquaintance with Jewish literature has revealed more fully the affinities he has with contemporary Jewish thought. Few things in the Epistles have been more richly illustrated from this source than his doctrine of angels and demons, which now stands before us in quite a new light. But I am less disposed than some scholars to rate the influence of contemporary Judaism high, at least so far as Paul's central doctrines are concerned. We have all too slender a knowledge of Judaism in Paul's day. The literary sources for the study of Rabbinic theology are much later, and the question arises how far we may use them for the reconstruction of a considerably earlier stage of thought. It may be plausibly argued that we can confidently explain coincidences with Paulinism much more readily on the assumption that Paul was the debtor. It is unlikely that the Rabbis consciously adopted Christian ideas. But this by no means settles the question. The amazingly rapid spread of Christianity quickly created a Christian atmosphere, in which it would not be unreasonable to suppose that Judaism itself experienced some modification. We know that there was considerable controversy between Jews and Christians. And we may well believe that its inevitable result would be that where Christians fastened on the weak points of Judaism and demonstrated the superiority of the Christian view, the Jew would be naturally tempted to change his ground and persuade himself that really these views were his own. It is also possible that we have commonly overestimated the hostility between the adherents of the two religions, and unduly underrated the extent to which friendly relations existed in the early period. In this way Christian influence may have filtered into contemporary Judaism. We have, however, a number of Jewish Apocalypses, earlier than Paul or roughly contemporary with him. These, it must be remembered, represent a peculiar tendency; how far Paul stood under its influence we hardly know. But where we find coincidences, Paul's indebtedness can hardly be denied. In determining the extent to which we can rely on later Rabbinical documents in reconstructing the Judaism of the first century, it must not be forgotten that the appalling catastrophes, which overwhelmed the Jewish race in the first and second centuries of our era, must have changed the conditions profoundly in the theological as well as the political world. The

THE QUINTESSENCE OF PAULINISM 121

Judaism of the later centuries was hardly identical with the Judaism in which Paul was trained.

At present it is fashionable to make much of Greek influence on Paul. Not so long ago one of the most eminent exponents of Paulinism explained it as a mixture of Rabbinical and Alexandrian Judaism, in which the incongruous elements were so badly blended that the theology contradicted itself on fundamental principles. Radical contradictions in the system of such a thinker as Paul are antecedently improbable and to be admitted only on cogent evidence. This verdict rests on no assumption as to Paul's inspiration, it is simply a tribute due to a thinker of the highest eminence. Alexandrian Judaism contained a large element of Greek philosophy. Nowadays, it is specially in Stoicism and the Greek mysteries that the source of much in the Pauline theology is discovered. The presence of Greek elements would not be in any way surprising. Paul was born and bred in a famous University city; he mixed freely with Greeks, converted and unconverted, in his evangelistic work. It would not have been astonishing that one who became a Greek to the Greeks should have incorporated in his theology ideas derived from Greek philosophy. I am by no means concerned to deny points of contact, but I believe that it is here as with Jewish theology, that these are to be found not so much in the centre as in the outlying regions of his theology. I may quote on this point the pronouncement of Harnack whose judgement is exceptionally weighty. He says, with reference to Paul: 'Criticism, which is today more than ever inclined to make him into a Hellenist (so e.g. Reitzenstein), would do well to gain at the outset a more accurate knowledge of the Jew and the Christian Paul before it estimates the secondary elements which he took over from the Greek Mysteries. It would then see at once that these elements could have obtruded themselves on him only as uninvited guests, and that a deliberate acceptance is out of the question.' I will illustrate this point from a notable instance in the last century. I choose this because it concerns the right interpretation of a crucial element in Paulinism. I have already explained why I cannot accept the view that Paul's doctrine of the flesh is to be interpreted through the Old Testament. Several scholars derived it from Greek philosophy, and among them the name of Holsten deserves special mention. He discovered in Paul's doctrine the Greek contrast between matter and spirit. The flesh he identified with the body, explaining that when the body was spoken of as 'flesh' the emphasis was on the material of which it was composed and when the flesh was spoken of as 'body' the stress lay on the form into which it was organized. It is very dubious if this interpretation can be successfully sustained in detailed exegesis. But, apart from that, there are more general difficulties which appear to me to be insuperable. In the first place Paul's language varies very significantly when he is speaking of the flesh and when he is speaking of the body. The flesh is so thoroughly vicious and so utterly hostile to God that Christianity does not redeem but crucifies it. But while the flesh is crucified, the body of the Christian is the temple of the Holy Ghost and destined to share in the spirit's immortality. Further, when Paul enumerates the works of the flesh he includes sins which are not physical, especially sins of temper. Again, his doctrine would surely have taken a very different turn if he had regarded the body as the seat of sin. The way of salvation would have lain through ascetism, a starving and a crushing of the body under the rule of the spirit. And I am not sure that a rigorous logic would not go still farther. If the body is the seat of sin then death is the means of redemption. And this would have had a twofold consequence, that while men were in the body they could not be free from sin, and on the other hand, that complete redemption might be at once secured by suicide. Now Paul drew neither of these conclusions; on the contrary it was a commonplace in his theology that while a man was in the body he might have ceased to be in the flesh. On these grounds I am compelled to reject the view that for Paul the flesh and the body were identical, and that his doctrine of the flesh embodies the antithesis of matter and spirit borrowed from Greek philosophy. And finally, as indicating how improbable it is that Paul should have derived his fundamental doctrines in general, and this in particular, from Greek philosophy, we have his whole treatment of the question of the resurrection. In discussing it he speaks as if the resurrection of the body and the extinction of being were the only two alternatives, and does not take into account the third possibility of the immortality of the disembodied spirit. The importance of this fact will be more clearly seen, when we remember that the Greek doctrine of immortality was closely connected with that view of matter as evil, and the antithesis of body and spirit which Paul is supposed to have derived from Greek philosophy. If he borrowed the one why should he be so unconscious of the other?

I pass on to the question of the relation of Paulinism to the teaching of Jesus. The view that Paul owed little to the teaching of Jesus was more fashionable at one time than it is today, though it still finds advocates. We are told that the apostle had but little interest in the earthly life of Jesus. His attention was fixed on the Pre-existence, the Incarnation, the Passion, the Resurrection, the Ascension, the Session at God's right hand. His thought and emotion were concentrated on these great theological facts; to the details of His earthly career and to His teaching he was almost entirely indifferent. Although the remarkable silence of the Pauline Epistles on the life and teaching of Jesus renders such a view plausible, I cannot believe that it will bear searching scrutiny. The extent of the silence may be exaggerated. Paul appeals to the sayings of Jesus as finally settling certain questions of conduct. His knowledge of the facts of Christ's career and the details of His teaching was probably more extensive than has often been admitted; and his attachment to His person, the depth of his gratitude to Him, were too profound for such indifference to be at all natural. I do not institute any detailed comparison between the utterances of Jesus and the epistles of His apostle, but I remind you of the situation in which Paul was placed. There is unquestionably a change in the centre of gravity. Paul's emphasis is thrown much more fully on the great facts of redemption, the Death and the Resurrection. This indeed is not unnatural. Jesus was naturally reticent as to the theological significance of facts, the possibility of which His disciples were unwilling to contemplate. And the Cross itself inevitably put the teaching into a secondary place. The deed of Jesus was mightier than His word. At first an insuperable objection to the acceptance of Him as Messiah, it had become for Paul the Divine solution of his problem, his deliverance from condemnation and from moral impotence. It contained a deeper revelation of God's nature and His love than the loftiest teaching of Jesus could convey. Here was the climax of God's slow self-disclosure, manifested not in words, however sweet, tender, and uplifting, but in a mighty act, which filled that teaching with wholly new depth and intensity of meaning. And if it is true that the greatest contribution which Jesus made to religion was just the personality of Jesus Himself and His supreme act of sacrifice, then Paul was right in placing the emphasis where he did, even though one might wish he had drawn more fully on the words of Jesus when writing his epistles. Those epistles, however, were written to Christian communities, the majority of them founded by Paul himself, and in any case in possession of a background of information as to Jesus. But the situation of Paul had a peculiarity which must never be overlooked in considering this question. However content he may have been with his own experience, however deeply convinced of its evidential value, he could not forget that it was incommunicable, and that his own bare word was insufficient to substantiate the truth of his message. Through much of his career he was on his defence against those who stigmatized him as no genuine exponent of the Gospel. The other apostles looked coldly on his presentation of Christianity. He had to fight the battle of Christian freedom not only against them but even against his own trusted comrade, Barnabas. His enemies followed him from church to church, to poison the minds of his converts against him. Is it conceivable that, placed in this situation Paul could have been indifferent to the life and teaching of the Founder? Even if he had not needed the knowledge for his own satisfaction, it was a strategic necessity to him. How could he have afforded to insist on his right to be a genuine apostle of Jesus, a true herald of His Gospel, if all the time he was presenting his opponents in the Judaizing controversy with the opening given to them by such ignorance and indifference? Often contrasted unfavourably with the other apostles, he could not have failed to diminish by diligent inquiry their advantage over him as companions and pupils of Jesus. We must infer therefore that he had an adequate knowledge of the historical facts and the Founder's teaching, whatever view we take as to the evidence of such knowledge afforded by the epistles.

Something he must have owed to the apostles, notably to Peter. Much of his knowledge of the facts of Christ's life, His Passion and His Resurrection would be derived from this source. He shared with them the belief in certain fundamental facts, but their agreement went beyond this point. There was an element of theological interpretation common to them. Paul explicitly mentions, not only the fact that Christ died, but the vital interpretation, which turned the fact into a Gospel, that Christ died for our sins. From them he derived the institutions of Baptism and the Lord's Supper and the expectation of Christ's speedy return. Yet Paul emphatically asserts that he did not receive his Gospel from man but that it came to him by revelation. His distinctive presentation of Christianity was accordingly original, not borrowed; and the fullest recognition of that fact is not incompatible with the admission that there was not a little in his thought which he owed to others. That which he received from others by no means accounted for Paulinism. It is not so difficult to accumulate parallels to this detail and that; what is not possible is to discover a parallel to the system as a whole. Views which Paul did not originate he treated in an original way, stamped them with his own genius, and fused them into harmony with his general point of view. He was a speculative thinker of no mean order, not the second-rate eclectic whom some would make him out to be.

Paul's original contribution to Christian theology grew directly out of his own experience. This will be most clearly seen if, so far as we can, we trace the development of that experience. He had been trained as a Pharisee in the most rigorous type of Judaism. He had sought for righteousness, for a right standing before God, with a burning passion and unflagging energy. The standard of righteousness had been laid down in the Law, and he sought to fashion his life in strict and punctilious conformity with it. He achieved such success that he could claim to have outstripped all his contemporaries in the pursuit of righteousness, and could describe himself as blameless with reference to the Law. Yet his efforts, so strenuous and outwardly so successful, left him with a sense of desires unsatisfied and a goal always unreached. In the classic fragment of autobiography that he has given us in Romans 7, he has sketched with inimitable insight and in graphic and telling language, his spiritual career while he was under the Law. It was the flesh that made him weak, sin had seized it and used it as a base of operations, had conquered and brought him into captivity. It had not always been so with him. He looked wistfully back to the time when he was alive in childish innocence, wholly unconscious of sin. From this he was roused by the coming of the Law into his life. Conscious now of the holy Law of God, he realized his own disharmony with it. Moreover he felt that the Law's prohibitions were turned by sin into suggestions of transgression. Such then was his bitter experience. He had lost his innocence, his happy unconsciousness of a moral order had given place to a sense of disunion with it; he felt himself sold in helpless and hopeless captivity to sin, and the fact that the Law forbade a certain course of action became, in this perversion of his moral nature, the very reason why he should follow it. But all this implied that a higher element was present within him; otherwise he could never have felt the wretchedness of his condition or been sensible of the tragic schism in his soul. Looking more deeply into himself, he realized that within his own personality competing powers struggled for supremacy. On the one side there was his lower nature to which he gives the name 'the flesh', wherein sin had lain in a sleep like that of death till the Law had come and provoked it into revolt. While the mind consented to the Law of God that it was good, it was overmatched by the flesh which constantly insisted on his disobedience to it. The utmost strain of effort never altered the inward conditions; the sense of defeat remained. Now, as a pious Jew, this state of things must have seemed inexplicable to him. With a conscientiousness so acute, a nature so strenuous, and an ethical standard pitched so high, a moral tragedy was inevitable. The fault could not rest with the Law of God which could set forth no unattainable ideal, and therefore it must lie in himself. And yet how could he be at fault, since in his zeal for righteousness nothing had been left undone? This experience became clear to him later and supplied him with a large section of his theology, but at this time it could only have been an insoluble puzzle.

Then he came into contact with the Christians, and was stirred to the depths by their proclamation of a crucified Messiah. Their preaching would fill him with abhorrence, for the curse of the Law rested on him who was hanged on a tree. It was not simply that the religious leaders of the nation had decided against Jesus; the decisive verdict had been given by God. It was conceivable, however improbable, that God's Messiah should have been executed; it was unthinkable that He should have been executed by such a death. The doctrine of a crucified Messiah was a blasphemous paradox. But if he pressed the Christians with the dilemma their position seemed to involve, they must have escaped it by their confident assertion that God Himself had intervened in the resurrection of the Crucified to vindicate His character and establish the truth of His claim. But they would not leave the death itself without an attempt at explanation. It was not for them simply an ugly and unwelcome incident, an inexplicable mystery, its burden lifted, but its obscurity unremoved, by the Resurrection. It was not an irrational accident violating the moral order; it was a deed that testified to the sin and ignorance of man, but also a part of God's plan for human redemption. But they did not realize, as Paul did, how fundamental were the problems which their position involved, and to what radical solution they must be carried if they maintained their belief in Jesus. Hate sharpened Paul's insight into the instability of their position, and it was his interest as a controversialist to push the logical conclusions from it to an extreme. With the swift intuition of genius he realized that to accept the Cross was to bid farewell to the Law. His ruthlessness as a persecutor is not to be palliated by the plea that he had failed to understand the Gospel. We may excuse it on the ground that he understood it so well. To a certain extent we may even say that one side of Paulinism was a theoretical construction formed by Paul in the period before he became a Christian. For if Jesus was indeed the Messiah, how did it stand with the Law? In condemning the Messiah, the Law condemned itself. But not on this ground alone would the acceptance of Christianity carry with it a renunciation of the Law. So tremendous a fact as the Messiah's death, and a death in this form, must have an adequate explanation. Such an explanation was actually given in the theory that the death of Jesus was to atone for sin and establish a new righteousness. It was obvious that a new righteousness through Christ would supplant the righteousness of the Law, and thus the privilege of the Jew disappeared and he sank to the level of the Gentiles.

Now, however strongly Paul pressed the Christians with the logic of their position, he could hardly help feeling as the controversy went on that his own position was not impregnable. He could not help being impressed by the constancy of the Christians under persecution, and the serenity with which they met their fate. Nor could he deny the possibility that their case might be true, however he despised and disbelieved it. As a Pharisee he could not reject the possibility of the Resurrection, nor evade the inference that it would neutralize the curse of the Law. The assertion that the Messiah had died to atone for sin was not intrinsically incredible, and it met very well the need of which he was himself conscious. To deny the fact of the Resurrection in face of the unwavering testimony of the Christians must have become always more difficult. Even while rejecting their belief as blasphemous, there was probably an undercurrent of uneasy questioning whether they might not be right after all. And this was strengthened by his consciousness of dissatisfaction with his own life under the Law, his realization that the Law had not brought him happiness, or assured him of his standing with God. Subconsciously at least it would seem probable that the issue had narrowed itself to this: Had Jesus risen from the dead or not? We may then sum up his position just before his conversion in this way: he passionately held fast the Law as God's appointed way of righteousness, but was conscious of inability on his own part to attain his ideal. For himself personally righteousness had not come through the Law. On the other hand he held Jesus to be a blasphemous pretender to Messiahship, cursed by the Law and therefore by God, but with misgivings whether after all He might not be the true Messiah; in which case His death was intended as an atonement for sin and to create that righteousness before God, which in Paul's own experience at least the Law had been unable to do. In which case again the Law was abolished, and Jew and Gentile were placed on the same level before God.

There came to Paul in this state of mind the overwhelming experience on the road to Damascus. The Nazarene, whom his countrymen had sent to the Cross and whose followers he had persecuted to the death, appeared to him in a blinding blaze of heavenly glory. In that experience the Pauline theology came to birth. The full and radiant conviction now and for ever possessed him, that the crucified Jesus had risen from the dead and now reigned in glory, and was therefore the Messiah whom He had proclaimed Himself to be. The inferences he had previously drawn in order to fortify himself in his rejection of Christianity and persecution of the Christians still held good. When he accepted Christianity, he accepted the conclusions which he had previously regarded as inevitable. Once for all he abandoned the belief that righteousness could come through the Law. He acquiesced in the abolition of the Law, which had pronounced its curse upon his Master, and he freely admitted the universality of salvation and the abolition of all distinction between Gentile and Jew. But theoretical inferences, drawn from the standpoint of Judaism, were wholly inadequate to express the fullness of blessing which had come to him in his conversion. The splendour of illumination which had flooded his soul was miraculous to him, matching the marvel of the light which burst on the primeval chaos, when God began to deliver the earth from darkness and disorder. It had brought to him the knowledge of God in the face of Jesus Christ. A description of his experience even more pregnant and suggestive is given in the Epistle to the Galatians: 'When it pleased God, who before my birth set me apart for His service and called me through His grace, to reveal His Son in me.' It would be vain to attempt a psychological analysis of the inmost fact in Paul's experience, and inquire in what way this revelation was imparted. But the words are full of significance. The passage carries us a long way into the heart of the Pauline theology. It was God who had taken the initiative in this great act of revelation. Thus the Gospel was not a wholly new thing. It did not make an absolute breach with the past but stood in continuity with it; it was the God of the Old Covenant who was also the God of the New. Thus Paul secured the inclusion of the Old Testament revelation in Christianity. His disciple Marcion at a later period rejected the God of the Jews and the Hebrew Scriptures, and regarded Christianity as a sudden irruption of the new order into the old without any preparation in history. For Paul the new religion proclaims the ancient God. And this God reveals His Son. Jesus is thus not merely a national Messiah. The Messianic category, true so far as it goes, is inadequate. Paul claims for Him a loftier title. Thus, while his monotheism remained, it was not a bare monotheism, but a monotheism which, while maintaining the unity of the Godhead, found room for distinctions within it. And this revelation was made within him. It is an inward revelation that the phrase is intended to express; and we can hardly be wrong in finding here his deepest experience in conversion, the vital and mystical union of his spirit with Christ Himself. But out of this certain consequences inevitably flow. If he was one with Christ then Christ's experiences had become his own, and Christ's resources were in a sense placed at his disposal. Thus he was free from the Law, and in Christ he stood righteous before God. And with the Law he had died in Christ to the flesh; and therefore to sin which, apart from the flesh, had no foothold in man. We may then summarize the positions held by Paul at his conversion or given in it as follows: Monotheism, qualified by the recognition of distinctions within the Godhead; the choice of Israel and revelation to it, qualified by the inability of the Law to produce righteousness; the reign of sin in the individual by means of the flesh, against which the struggles of the mind were quite ineffectual; the recognition of righteousness as a free gift of God apart from the merit or effort of the recipient; the union of the human spirit with Christ, the crucified and risen Lord; and through this union the forgiveness of sins, victory over sin, and power for a new life.

From this sketch of Paul's spiritual history we must now pass on to a more systematic and detailed exposition of his fundamental doctrines. We must of course remember that his recognition of a Divine revelation already given to Israel compelled him to adjust to the Old Testament as best he could the theology derived from experience. His experience before conversion, interpreted in the light of the Gospel, shaped his doctrines of sin, the flesh, and the Law. Of the flesh I have spoken already when considering the alleged derivation of Paul's conception from the Old Testament and Greek philosophy. On it therefore I need add only a few words. In his experience the flesh had been the seat and the instrument of sin. Apart from the flesh there could be no sin in man. Flesh without sin was also unknown. Now the flesh, unlike the body, is not a morally indifferent thing, which may become the slave of sin or the temple of the Holy Ghost. It is completely antagonistic to God and righteousness. In it there dwells no good thing; it has a will and intent which leads to death; it lusts against the spirit; cannot be subject to God's law. Its works are altogether evil, and exclude those who practise them from the kingdom of God. Those whose life is lived in accordance with it are inevitably on the way to death; and those who sow to it will of it reap corruption. Those who are in the flesh cannot please God. This dark and lurid picture shows us clearly how irretrievably evil a thing Paul considered the flesh to be.

But reflection on his own experience had taught him to find in the Law the stimulus which wakened this hateful impulse to its malign activity. In this he detected one of the darkest shades in the character of sin. Nothing brought out its true heinousness more clearly than this that it perverted into an instrument of its baneful energy God's holy law itself. Thus the Law could not secure obedience because it was weak through the flesh, while it proved in experience to be the strength of sin. So there emerges one of the most paradoxical features in the Pauline theology. It would have seemed as though there could be but one answer to the question,

Why had the Law been given to Israel? For what purpose could it have been given, save to teach man the way of righteousness, and guide and stimulate him as he sought to tread it? But though such was its obvious design, Paul felt that in his own career it had failed to achieve it. It would not have been so strange had he simply said that the Law was given to convince man of his own sinfulness by setting before him a moral ideal of which he fell lamentably short. But he goes farther than this and teaches that it was given for the sake of transgression, and came in besides that the trespass might abound. We must, it is true, maintain the distinction between sin and trespass, and not understand him to mean that the Law was given in order that sin might be increased. It was in order that the sin already latent in man should reveal itself in its true colours through abundant manifestation in acts of transgression. Such he had found it to be. He says: 'I was alive apart from the Law once: but when the commandment came, sin sprang to life and I died.' In his innocent childhood, when he was just a creature of impulse and knew the restraint of no moral law, he lived his happy untroubled life, conscious of no schism within his own breast. But when he came to years of moral discernment, and realized that he was placed in a moral order, the flesh chafed at its pressure, and the sin which had been slumbering in it woke to life and disclosed its native antagonism to God. Thus the Law, holy, just, and good, so framed that obedience to it would have brought life and righteousness, had issued in condemnation and death. It had brought the consciousness of sin, it had become its strength and stronghold. Thus Paul is led to the paradoxical doctrine that the Law had not been intended to produce righteousness, but to produce the effects, which it had in fact achieved. God had meant it to give sin its opportunity, to prove an incentive to transgression. It is not strange that Jewish writers, for whom the Law is not an intolerable yoke and brings not a curse but a blessing, should criticize Paul's doctrine as utterly contrary to the facts. Indeed we can hardly wonder that some should doubt whether anyone capable of formulating it could ever have known Judaism from the inside. Yet it is not difficult to see how Paul was driven to take up this position. It is one of those cases where the necessity of adjustment to the Old Testament has shaped the doctrine which yet it did not create. There is nothing to show that he ever contemplated the solution adopted by Marcion that Judaism with its

Law and Old Testament Canon should be frankly abandoned. We cannot doubt that he would have utterly repudiated it. But, realizing that Christianity stood in continuity with Judaism, and that for it too the Old Testament was sacred Scripture, and that the Law had actually been given by God, though through angelic intermediaries, he had the difficult task of combining his conviction of its Divine origin with the fact that it had proved to be the strength of sin. He solved his difficulty by the bold contention that the Law had never been intended to bring righteousness, for God could not have adopted a means so ill designed to serve His end. Now it may be urged that this is just a piece of desperate apologetic, to which Paul would never have been driven but for a certain morbid strain in his own piety. With a conscience more robust, less scrupulous and sensitive, he might have had a happier life under the Law, more free from incessant strain and sense of failure. And no doubt it is true that Paul's case was quite exceptional. Yet the following considerations must be borne in mind. Paul as we know him in his epistles is remarkably sane and balanced in his handling of ethical questions. It is not easy to believe that the man who holds the scales so evenly between the strong and the weak, who shows himself so conscious of the merits and perils of both, should himself have been the victim of a too scrupulous, not to say diseased, conscience. Further it may be freely granted that in multitudes of instances legalism worked well. Judaism could point, and can point, to a noble roll of saints and martyrs. Yet legalism is not, I believe, the highest type of religious experience; and the defects which Paul believed it had shown in his own case are such as might have been theoretically deduced. A legal religion may with shallower natures produce self-satisfaction on too low a level of attainment, while in the more strenuous and sensitive it may create a depressing sense of failure. With Paul this depression passed into despair. Are we unjust to others if we say that this was rooted in a wholly exceptional realization of the lofty standard which the Law challenged him to reach, and a keener sense of his own shortcomings? Surely, remembering that Paul is one of the greatest personalities in history, a religious genius who ranks among the foremost of his order, we may hesitate before we dismiss his judgement on the Law with the cheap explanation that Paul was the victim of ethical nightmare.

His doctrine of salvation and the new life is similarly an interpretation of his own experience. I have already expressed the opinion that when Paul uses the words 'it pleased God to reveal His Son in me' he was speaking of that mystical union with Christ, which was fundamental in his doctrine as it was central in his experience. This is not merely a moral union, that is a union of will and thought. Such a union of course is involved; he wills the things which Christ wills and judges as He judges. But the union of which Paul speaks is deeper and more intimate; it is a blending of personalities in which, while in a sense the personalities remain distinct, in another sense they are one. To express a merely moral union he must have chosen other language. The language he actually uses would be too extravagant. Christ is in the believer, the believer in Christ. He that is joined to the Lord is one spirit. Paul even says: 'I have been crucified with Christ, and it is no longer I that live, but Christ liveth in me.' He has transcended the narrow limits of his personality, and become one with a personality vaster and more universal. He has been lifted into a larger life, and in that life he has found an answer to the problems which had been insoluble. As one with Christ he makes his own the experience through which Christ has passed. He suffers with Christ, he is nailed to His Cross, he dies and rises with Him, he sits with Him in the heavenly places. He shares Christ's status before God, His character, and His destiny. In Christ he is a new creature; the old life with its claims and its sin, its guilt and its condemnation, has passed away and all is new. The secret of this mystical union is hidden from us in the thick darkness where God dwells. It is an ultimate fact of experience which admits of no further analysis.

In his life under the Law Paul had a passion for righteousness, that is for a right standing before God. But he was conscious that he fell short of what God required, and was not justified as he stood at God's bar. But having passed from the old life to the new he realized that because he was one with Christ, Christ's righteousness was his. He was justified or acquitted or pronounced righteous in Christ; or to put the thought in its negative form, there was no condemnation for him. The verdict God utters on Christ, He utters on those who are identified with Him. This doctrine of justification is of course important, but it is secondary rather than primary; it is part of his larger doctrine of mystical union. And when we understand this we have the answer to the criticism that the doctrine involves a fiction and is therefore immoral. To pronounce the sinner righteous is apparently a fiction. But this does no justice to Paul's meaning. The act of trust creates the mystical union and it is the new man, who is one with Christ, on whom the verdict of justification is pronounced. Union with Christ creates the new character which requires the new status. Paul was conscious that the life in harmony with God's will, which he had sought to gain by the works of the Law, had become his possession without effort of his own. And he shares also in Christ's blessed immortality. To these points I must return in connexion with the larger aspects of the theology.

These larger aspects we may consider as Paul's philosophy of history. This also is intimately associated with his experience. He starts from the individual, from himself, and regards his own history as typical. As he had sinned and found salvation, so had others. But he was not content till, with the philosopher's instinct, he had pressed behind the multifariousness of phenomena to a principle of unity. The individual he generalizes into a racial experience. He explains sin and redemption through the acts of Adam and Christ. The moulds into which his thought is poured were given him by history, yet his doctrine is essentially a philosopher's generalization of experience.

I do not accept the view that Paul attached little importance to his doctrine of Adam, since he introduces it incidentally and as an illustration of the act of Christ. It was rather of fundamental importance. To do it justice we must detach ourselves completely from modern interpretations. We must not read Romans in the light of the story of Eden, nor yet the story of Eden in the light of Romans. The ideas are quite different in the two passages. Nor must we suppose that the validity of the Pauline doctrine depends on the historicity of the story in Genesis. Unquestionably Paul took that story to be literal history, nothing else could be reasonably expected from him. What I find remarkable, however, is that substantially his doctrine is so constructed as to be unaffected by our answer to the question whether the narrative of the Fall is history or myth. So far as Adam has any significance for Paul it is not Adam as a mere individual, but as one who is in a sense the race. It is surely improbable that Paul could have been content to regard the whole of humanity as committed by the accidental act of one unit in its many millions. To assign such momentous significance to the arbitrary and the capricious, would be to take the control of history out of the hands of reason. For him Adam is typical of the race. He does not think of man's moral nature as damaged by the act of Adam, nor does he suppose that the moral status of humanity is fixed by what was nothing more than the act of an irresponsible individual. What alone could rightly make the act of Adam the act of the race, stamping humanity as good or evil, would be an identity of Adam with the race, so that in his acts the whole quality of humanity is manifest. The act of Adam is crucial just because it is typical; the nature of Adam is our common nature; he is the natural man, moulded from the dust. The sin latent in us was latent also in him, and at the touch of the Law it was roused to life and activity. Only because Adam was truly representative, could the individual act be charged with universal significance. His act involved God's judgement of the race as sinful, and brought on all men the penalty of death. Such is the tragic history of the natural man left to himself. But it was not from the Old Testament in the first instance that Paul learnt this doctrine, as will be clear to anyone, if he does not read the third of Genesis through Pauline spectacles. Closer parallels may, it is true, be found in Jewish theology. But it was his own experience that was his starting-point. We should read the discussion of Adam and Christ in the light of the autobiographical fragment in the seventh of Romans. As he pondered on the conflict within his own nature, the struggle between the flesh and the mind, the victory of sin, the impotence of the Law for righteousness, its capture by sin for its own evil ends, he sought the explanation at the fountain head of history. In his own heart he found the key to the long tragedy of man's sin and guilt. As he was so was mankind. His own breast was a tiny stage on which the vast elemental conflict of good and evil was re-enacted. So had it been with the first man, so from the very outset of the race's history at the touch of the Law the sin that slumbered in the flesh had sprung to consciousness and revolt. And all the generations, as they came and went, had but vindicated by their universal transgression God's treatment of that first disobedience as a racial act.

But before the second racial personality could come, and by his act reverse the verdict on humanity and release new streams of energy to cleanse and redeem it and lift it from the natural to the spiritual plane, a long interval had to elapse. Another pair of contrasted figures, Abraham and Moses, play a subordinate part in the drama. With the former is associated the promise of the Seed and the election of Israel, with the latter the Law. Against those who claimed that the Law was permanent and not abolished by the Gospel that both it and circumcision were essential to justification, Paul urges the case of Abraham. Long before the Law was given, the promise of God had been made to Abraham, a promise of the Seed in whom all nations should be blest, a promise fulfilled in the Gospel. But the very principles of the Gospel were already in operation, for Abraham was justified by faith and not by works, and while he was still uncircumcised. And the promise by its very nature offered a contrast to the Law. For Law has within it an element of bargain, the performance of its demand implies a corresponding right to receive a reward. But the promise stands on the higher plane of free grace; it guarantees a gift bestowed by God's bounty apart from any desert in the recipient. The promise then is not only more ancient than the Law and cannot be superseded by it, it belongs also to a loftier moral order. And with the promise there comes the election, the choice of Abraham's descendants. But not of all of them; for the principle of election still works on, choosing Isaac and Jacob, passing by Ishmael and Esau. And in the chosen people itself it still works; not all of Israel after the flesh constitutes the spiritual Israel. The Old Testament more than once speaks of a remnant, and now the Israel of God is identical with the Christian Church. Yet the natural Israel is not ultimately rejected, for Paul looks forward to the time when it shall accept its Messiah, and form part of the elect people once more.

But why, it may be asked, if already in Abraham the principles of the Gospel found expression, could not the Messiah have come at once, and why was there any need for the Law? It was because a prolonged period of discipline was necessary to educate the chosen people and prepare for the coming of the Messiah. The weakness of human nature had to be revealed by its inability to fulfil the Law, so too, the ineradicable vice of the flesh and the exceeding sinfulness of sin. It was only the Law that could disclose the mutinous character of the flesh, or wake to evil activity the sin that was dormant within it. But while on the one hand the Law disclosed to man his true nature and exhibited sin in its true colours, it also served as moral discipline. It revealed man's duty, though it gave no power to fulfil it. It was a 'paidagogos' to bring us to Christ. The paidagogos was charged with the moral supervision of children. By the use of this term Paul suggests the menial and temporary character of the Law. Israel was like a child in its tutelage under harsh and ungenial tutors. But with the coming of Christ the period of bondage is over, the heir achieves his freedom, and passes into that liberty for which Christ has set him free. The Law itself by its very imperfections pointed forward to Christ; it set before man a moral ideal, and since it gave no power to fulfil its own commands and was the weak, unwilling tool of sin, it pointed to a new revelation, in which the moral ideal should be united with the power of fulfilment.

In the fullness of time the promise, so long obstructed by the Law, came to realization. God sent His Son into the world in the likeness of sinful flesh, a member of the human race and of the Hebrew people. He did not begin to be with His human origin; a heavenly life lay behind His life of humiliation and suffering on earth. Image of the invisible God, firstborn of creation, sharing the Divine essence, God's agent in the formation of the universe, He did not clutch greedily at that equality with God, which was nevertheless His right, but emptied Himself and for our sake exchanged His heavenly riches for our earthly poverty. Stooping to our human estate He obediently accepted the Cross which God appointed Him, and has in recompense been highly exalted and received the name above every name.

While the act of Adam had been critical and representative, since it expressed our common nature, the act of Christ was a critical and racial act in virtue of His self-identification with us. As Adam in this crucial act is the race, so also in His crucial act is Christ; and as the act of one is valid for the race, so also is the act of the other. Each of them is the fountain-head of humanity, the one of the natural, the other of the redeemed. Their significance is not merely individual, it is universal. The point of expression is in each case personal; it is Adam who eats the forbidden fruit, it is Jesus of Nazareth who hangs upon the Cross. But when viewed not from the standpoint of historical incident but of eternal significance, Adam and Christ are co-extensive with humanity.

Yet the question emerges whether we can rightly draw a parallel between the racial function of the first and the second Adam. Obviously they do not seem to stand in the same relation to the body for which they act. There is clearly no such hereditary connexion in the one case as obtains in the other. But it is not on the hereditary connexion that Paul's thought rests, but on the possession of a common nature. Yet is there not a difference here also? The act of Adam was not in violation of his nature, it sprang spontaneously from it; and it was a racial act because his nature and that of all other men were identical. There is, it is true, a higher element than the flesh within us, but it makes no successful stand against the lower. In Christ, on the contrary, the higher element is all powerful; He is the spiritual man of heavenly origin. Here then, it might seem, that the parallel between the two Adams breaks down, since while a natural man might fitly represent the sinful race, a spiritual man could not do so. On this the following suggestions may be offered. In the first place Paul does hint at an essential relation subsisting between the pre-existent Christ and the human race. In the next place the element of spirit is not absent even from sinful humanity, so that what is needed is not so much the introduction of a new element as such a readjustment of the old as shall emancipate the higher nature from the dominion of the lower. And thirdly, if such a readjustment is not only realized in Christ but through Him becomes possible to the race and to individuals, He may be regarded as acting for the race with as much right as Adam. In fact the 'much more' which rings so loudly in Paul's great passage on Adam and Christ is perhaps the key to this difficulty. Christ acts for the race not simply because He shares its nature and its fortunes, but because there dwells within Him a spring of redemptive energy, which makes it possible for the achievements He accomplishes in His own case, to be repeated in the experience of the race and of individuals. We need to hold fast as our guiding clue not simply that Christ reverses all that Adam did, but that He much more than reverses it.

But what was the significance of Christ's racial act? Paul describes it as an act of obedience. As such it reversed Adam's act of disobedience and the consequences that followed from it. These consequences Paul took to be the penalty of physical death and Divine condemnation of the race as guilty. Through the obedience of Christ, physical death is cancelled by the resurrection of the body, and God now passes a new judgement on the race as He sees it in Christ. The act of Christ stood also in a relation to the old order under which men had lived. That order had been under the control of inferior spiritual powers. There was a kingdom of evil with Satan the god of this world, the prince of the power of the air at its head. Still the Christian finds that his 'wrestling is not against flesh and blood, but against the principalities, against the powers, against the world-rulers of this darkness, against the spiritual *hosts* of wickedness in the heavenly *places*'. Clad in the armour of God he may be able to withstand the wiles of the devil, and equipped with the shield of faith to quench all the fiery darts of the evil one. Behind the whole system of idolatry Paul sees the baneful activity of the demons; to them the heathen sacrifices are offered, and the Christian who feasts in the idol's temple enters into ruinous fellowship with demons. But there were also the angels. It is not easy for us to enter into Paul's thought here. Paul's conception of angels has been borrowed from Jewish theology, and it has little in common with our popular notions of angels. They are the elemental spirits who rule the present world. They are not sinless, they have shared in the effects of Christ's redemption and therefore need to be redeemed. They are to stand before the judgement bar of the saints. Women are in danger from them if they pray or prophesy in the Christian assemblies with uncovered head, and therefore need the protection of the veil, to which a magical power is often assigned. In particular the angels had been concerned with the giving of the Law. This was a tenet of Jewish theology and references are made to it in the speech of Stephen and in the Epistle to the Hebrews; while Paul accepts the belief in the Epistle to the Galatians, and it underlies much that is said in the Epistle to the Colossians. The angels, as the world-rulers, brought Christ to His Cross, for they are absorbed in their function and have no significance beyond it. If then there rests on Jesus the condemnation and the curse of the Law, when we pass from the abstract to the concrete, the responsibility rests with those who are the givers and administrators of the Law. And these are not primarily the Jewish or Roman authorities. Just as behind the Empires of Persia and Greece the Book of Daniel shows us their angelic princes, so angelic principalities and powers stand behind their human tools, the priest and the procurator. They act not in malevolence but in ignorance. Had they known the wisdom of God, they would not have crucified the Lord of glory. The ignorance of the angels is mentioned also in the Epistle to the Ephesians. Through the Church the variegated wisdom of God is to be divulged to the principalities and powers in the heavenly places. But their action in bringing Christ to His Cross recoiled upon themselves. The Law launched its curse against Christ, but in doing so its curse was exhausted and its tyranny was broken. In His death Christ spoiled the principalities and powers, exhibited them in their true position of inferiority, and led them in triumph in His train. Foolishly then did the false teachers at Colossae worship these deposed potentates and look to them for help. For the fullness of Godhead is not distributed among a multitude of angels. It exists in its undivided totality in Christ, it dwells in Him as a body, that is as an organic whole.

But while the Law has thus been abolished by being nailed to Christ's cross, sin and the flesh have also been brought to nought. For the crucifixion of the physical flesh carries with it the destruction of the carnal nature. And similarly the death of Christ broke the dominion of sin. For while the sinful flesh was crucified, the sin which dwelt within it was done away. Thus the death of Christ was a death to sin. And just as the physical death, so also the physical resurrection was the efficient symbol of a spiritual fact. The one broke with the past, the other inaugurated the future. The resurrection involved the resurrection to a new life. The negative death to sin is completed by the positive life unto God. And what Christ thus achieved, the race achieved in Him. It atoned for its sin, broke loose from its power, and was pronounced righteous as it stood before the bar of God.

So far, then, I have spoken of the two great racial acts. I have pointed out already that Paul traces certain consequences to these acts, which automatically affect the whole race apart from any individual choice. But other consequences, and these more momentous, depend on such choice. As a matter of historical fact, all men have by personal choice endorsed the act of Adam and made it their own, and thus vindicated the treatment of it as a racial act. But all do not by a similar act of choice so endorse the racial act of Christ and make it their own. It lies within the option of the individual whether he will remain a natural man, and live in the flesh on the level of Adam, or whether he will take his stand with Christ and become a spiritual man. If he does so, then by an act of faith he becomes one with Christ. Faith is a very rich idea with Paul, it is that act of personal trust and self-surrender, the movement of man's whole soul in confidence toward Christ, which makes him one spirit with Him. And thus the great racial act of Calvary is repeated in the believer's experience. Because he is one with Christ he is dead to sin; for the flesh in which it lived and through which it worked has been crucified on Christ's cross. He has also in death paid the penalty of his sin, and is thus free from its guilt and its claim. And since he is one spirit with Christ he has risen to the new life of holiness, and there works within him the power of Christ's resurrection life. No condemnation rests upon him before God's bar, he is justified in Christ. Thus not only sin and the flesh but the Law also has passed away. For where the Spirit of the Lord is, there is liberty; and Christians have died to the Law in which they were holden. For they have escaped into the freedom of the Spirit and dwell with Christ at the right hand of God. Christ has taken the place of self as the deepest and inmost element in their personality; they have been crucified with Christ and it is no longer they that live but Christ that liveth in them. Conduct thus ceases to be the studied and even painful adjustment to an external code of laws. It is the joyful, instinctive, spontaneous expression of the new personality. With the abolition of the Law the great barrier between Jew and Gentile has been broken down and Christianity stands revealed as a universal religion.

At present, it is true, the Christian realizes that his redemption is incomplete. What is ideally concentrated in the ecstatic moment of vision and emancipation, may in actual experience be achieved only through a tedious process. And complete redemption is not possible till the consummation. At present we groan beneath our burden; and all Nature moans also, looking eagerly for final redemption. At present we have but the earnest of the Spirit, but this is the pledge that all His fullness will be granted to us. For God, who did not spare His beloved Son but freely surrendered Him for our sakes, cannot withhold any good from us. If the status of Christ and His character become ours, we must share also His blessed immortality and His heavenly reign.

The secret of the spell which the theology of Paul has cast on such multitudes is to be found in the illumination which it has brought to their own spiritual history. They have understood their bondage and their deliverance, their misery and their rapture, as they have entered into his despair or watched him as he passed from that strain of inward conflict and sense of failure to harmony of spirit and untroubled peace with God. A theology created by experience speaks with directness and power to those whose pilgrimage has taken them along the same way. The influence of Paul ebbs and flows across long stretches of history. It shrinks and seems as if it would vanish and then all suddenly it gathers volume and velocity and the arid waste becomes a garden of God.

IV—ECCLESIASTICAL

THE REUNION OF THE CHRISTIAN CHURCHES[1]

WHEN I accepted this high honour and grave responsibility, it was my hope that I might speak of those central themes which lie nearer to the heart and deeper in the convictions of Christendom than those issues which range us in opposing camps. It is not in my temperament to love controversy, and I shrink from it most of all when it is controversy with my fellow-Christians. I dwell with far more contentment on those truths which unite us all in wonder and adoration, than on those questions which force us to take sides against each other, even if by the grace of God they do not cool the warmth of our affection and esteem. I am more concerned to expound eternal principles than to concentrate attention on topics of acute but transient interest. But the fates have been too strong for me. I cannot evade the challenge of the present situation. Yet I would face the problems of the passing moment in the light of those principles which are untouched by change.

Four places have been much in our minds—Lambeth, Malines, Lausanne, Westminster. The first three of these raised the question of Reunion explicitly; and the decision of Westminster may have profound reactions on the future of Home Reunion. We cannot do justice to the Church of England in any one of these unless we remember the peculiar position in which it stands. If it has affinities with the Lutheran, the Reformed, and our own Evangelical Churches, it has affinities on the other side with the Eastern and Latin Churches. Very many Anglicans believe that this position has been assigned to their Church by Providence, and that it is an instrument by which the Reunion of Christendom may be facilitated. If, then, it insists on conditions which we find distasteful, it is not from any spirit of arrogance, but largely because surrender might create insuperable difficulties for Reunion with the Eastern

[1] The Presidential Address delivered at the 33rd Annual Assembly of the National Free Church Council, 1928.

Orthodox Churches and with Rome. The problem, it must be remembered, is not simply one of Home Reunion.

The Lambeth Appeal was a noble document, comprehensive in its scope, lofty in its spirit, generous in its temper. The Christian Church owes much to the influential committee which drafted it, and especially to its Chairman, the Archbishop of York. I cannot recount the stages which followed its publication. But a committee of the Federal Council of the Evangelical Free Churches selected a few of its number to act as a joint sub-committee with a small number of Anglican representatives under the chairmanship of the Archbishop of York. Of this body I was myself a member. We held seventeen meetings. Our purpose was to explore the whole territory involved and see what solutions of the many difficult problems could be suggested. We were not in sight of negotiations, for which indeed we had no mandate. We spared no pains, however, to discover and understand each other's position and see if any way could be found to heal the wounds created by our division. There was no desire on either side to force the pace. We were convinced, indeed, that any attempt to push matters forward with undue speed would retard rather than hasten the consummation. We had to report to the full committee, the full committee to the Federal Council, the Federal Council to the appointing Churches, with which alone the possibility of action rested.

Throughout negotiations for Union it is incumbent on the Free Churches to remember that in constituting a united English Church our existing relations with Churches outside of England ought not to be impaired. The chief difficulty in creating such a Church arises in connexion with the ministry. It is recognized on the Anglican side that the ministry of the regularly constituted Free Churches is a true ministry within the Church of Christ. But from the Anglican point of view Episcopacy must be retained in the United Church, because its abandonment would not only be the surrender of something which all value highly and very many regard as essential, but it would snap one of the chief links with the Eastern and Roman communions. This condition, is, however, qualified by the proviso that it must be constitutional and not prelatical, and that it shall be combined with elements of congregational and presbyterial order. To an Episcopate so limited, provided no theory that Episcopacy is of the essence of the Church is demanded, I should personally have no objections. Church order is for me a matter of expediency and not of principle. I could live and work happily under any form of Church order except a despotism. The existing Anglican system needs strengthening and reform; but recent non-episcopal developments suggest a recognition that Episcopacy has its own value.

Far more serious is the problem of the ministry. The Free Church ministry, while real, is not regarded as qualified to consecrate the Eucharist in the Anglican rite. A Eucharist so consecrated would for a large number of Anglicans be invalid; the central act of worship and the supreme nourishment of the Christian life would be nullified. The recognition of its validity by the authorities of the Church of England would precipitate a schism.

How can this be met? Ordination pure and simple would be generally rejected by Free Churchmen because of the implication that their previous ministry was not real. In conditional ordination the assumption would rather be that it was real. Like conditional baptism for converts to Rome it would serve to guard against the possibility of defect and secure a satisfactory guarantee for those to whom the recipient would henceforth be qualified to minister. The Anglicans would on their part be prepared to accept a similar qualification which might commend their ministry to Free Churchmen. This seems to me radically distinct from a demand for ordination because it does not question the validity of the previous ordination; it is not, at least in intention, one-sided; and it would be designed to reassure anxious souls that the recipient could truly effect whatever they may believe that a minister does effect in the Eucharistic service. I could not accordingly condemn anyone who, moved by a desire for Reunion and to meet the tender conscience of others, accepted this additional qualification. But the general sentiment of Free Churchmen would, at present, not favour this solution. A third suggestion is that we should avoid the mixture of rites. Naturally if Reunion took place, the commission henceforth received at their ordination by all ministers in the United Church would qualify them for ministry throughout the Church. But those who were already in the ministry would continue to minister according to their previous practice in those sections of the Church in which they had previously been qualified to minister. This solution has the advantage that it would probably violate no convictions. But it would make the interim period abnormally long, and hamper that free circulation throughout the body which it is the object of Reunion to promote. On the other hand a generation or even two generations are not long in the life of a Church; and to gain so great a result this real inconvenience might cheerfully be borne.

But if the Anglicans could recognize that the essence of what is conveyed in ordination is authorization to minister in the ordaining body, then those who were already ministers in the respective Churches would need nothing more than reciprocal authorization to minister throughout the United Church. No question would be raised as to the reality of the previous ministry; there would simply be an extension of the sphere in which this ministry could be practised. To such a solution no objection in principle could be raised, for if ordination makes a man a minister in the universal Church, it nevertheless confers no authorization to minister in any communion but his own. Such a solution would be far preferable to those already mentioned. It is doubtful, however, if Anglo-Catholics would be generally willing to allow that it was enough.

Since the Lambeth Appeal was addressed to all Christian people, the Malines Conversations were quite in order.[1] The episode has shown how far toward Rome some Anglican scholars of eminence are prepared to go, and also how immovable the Papacy is. To this general question I must return.

The Lausanne Conference[2] was a most remarkable achievement since it included the Eastern Orthodox Church. Had Rome consented to participate it would have been a miracle. From all parts of the globe, from every main section of the Church, apart from Rome, representatives were present. That they could not join together at the Lord's table lay in the very nature of the case. But it was all to the good that they should not only discuss their differences in a frank and friendly way, but that they should unite in common acts of worship. Positive results were not wanting; but even more important was the atmosphere of our gatherings, their temper and spirit. In spite of their inability to share in our resolutions, the Eastern representatives did not break away; they took their part in our discussions and our worship. If the present results seem to be small, they are all we could have

[1] Conversations initiated between the Archbishop of Canterbury and Cardinal Mercier (1921–5). See *Documents on Christian Unity*, ed. G. K. A. Bell, First Series, pp. 349–65; Second Series, pp. 21–35.—Ed.

[2] World Conference on Faith and Order, Lausanne, 3rd–21st August 1927. —Ed.

reasonably anticipated; their future results may well be incalculable.

On Westminster I need not dwell at this point, the story is too familiar and the issue is still in debate.[1] But at two points we are specially concerned, the alleged Romeward tendency of the regulations for the Eucharist; and the possible clash between Church and Parliament, making the establishment a political issue of the first order.

I have touched but briefly on Malines, Lausanne, and Westminster because all in their own way raise problems which are best dealt with in a systematic discussion.

I stand with those who deplore our divisions and desire with all their hearts that the shattered unity of Christ's Church might be restored. I think of our separations as 'unhappy divisions', though I recognize that under present circumstances some combinations would be unhappier still. I would have a unity in which the greatest elasticity should be not simply permitted but welcomed. Every variety of organization, every shade of belief consistent with loyalty to our central affirmations, every type of worship congenial to our varied temperaments, should find in such a Church its legitimate home. Let us remind ourselves at the outset that our protests against positions we believe to be false, however necessary such protests may be, almost inevitably narrow us. We tend to push them into the centre instead of keeping them in their place. Then our emphasis is wrongly distributed, our presentation of the perfect orb of truth is distorted. We may regard views and usages as matters of principle, when we are really invoking that sacred name for our prejudices or our habits. There are indeed fixed principles, permanent characteristics, which must abide through all flux and change. But Free Churchmen may make the mistake of the Bourbons if, forgetting that all life involves development, adjustment to environment, they insist, as a matter of principle, on retaining their organization in its traditional form.

We can stereotype no stage in the Church's history—primitive Church, undivided Church, Western Church, or any later development. Our languid zeal, our faltering convictions, may indeed gain new life as we touch the bones of Elisha; but the dead hand of illustrious leaders may imprison us in the obsolete past and fetter

[1] Discussions on the Revised Prayer Book (1927-8). The Book was rejected by the House of Commons June 1928.—Ed.

us for effective service in the present. We are most loyal to the leaders of the past—our mid-Victorian leaders included—not when we debase their watchwords of the past into shibboleths for the present, but when we ask how the principles we share with them are to be applied to a novel situation. If I take a Laodicean view of certain questions which excite a burning interest in others, it is partly perhaps because I have no ecclesiastical character to lose, partly because the problems seem to be before us in a new form, which, while it leaves our principles intact, does demand a reconsideration of their application.

In particular, I trust we have broken with the view that a form of organization is right as it corresponds with the primitive model. Our interest in early Church organization is antiquarian. Congregationalism and Presbyterianism can, it is true, appeal to the Apostolic Age with better right that monarchical episcopacy. But no appeal to the first century can lawfully determine what our own organization should be. Deism in any form ought to be repulsive to us who believe in the Holy Ghost and the living Christ and are mindful of the warning that we must not seek the living among the dead. No form of organization has any intrinsic divine right. The living Church has the competence to create its own organization and to modify it by retrenchment here and expansion there, as new occasions arise and new needs have to be met.

Since the thorniest problems of Reunion emerge in connexion with the Church, its organization, its ministry, and its sacraments, we may begin with a consideration of these. In discussing the Church we are in the region of first principles and an appeal to the classical documents of our religion is altogether in place. They set before us a very lofty ideal. The Church is the Body and the Bride of Christ and the Holy Temple of God. Its members constitute an organic whole, a Body of which Christ is the Head. He is the principle of its unity; His life fills the whole organism and animates and controls all its members; His life-blood courses through its veins. It is the organ through which He functions in this lower world and exercises His gracious ministry. It is His Bride, the cherished object of His illimitable love, redeemed at the cost of His life; sadly stained and scarred at present, but destined for eternal fellowship with Him when He has presented it to Himself, pure and radiant, free from spot or wrinkle or any such thing. It is the Temple in which God dwells, which He hallows by His presence, wherein He is worshipped and where He and man can meet. Its unity should be marred by no schism, its loyalty compromised by no illicit love, its altar desecrated by no wilfulness or self-love. Such is the noble churchmanship of Paul; such and no meaner should be our own.

It is vital to insist that only when we have given its rightful position to the Church can we safely formulate any doctrine of the ministry. As a High Churchman I view with deep repugnance and distrust any theory of the ministry which tends to lower the conception of the Church. The unbalanced exaltation of the ministry may lead to the depression of the laity, the denial of the universal priesthood and the consequent depreciation of the Church as a whole. The cure for high clericalism is High Churchmanship; the antidote to extravagant claims for a section is an exalted conception of the whole body. Apart from the Church the ministry is nothing at all. It possesses significance only as it serves the Church and enables it to function more effectively. The ministry has nothing which the whole body does not possess, though functions which belong to the Church as a whole may be fitly exercised by a special order. But should the body be totally deprived of its ministry it can replace it out of its own resources.

The minister must have his own individual call from God. But the commission to exercise his office must come to him through the Church. The head does not act without the body. The minister may not go over the head and behind the back of the Church to Christ. His vocation must be tested and proved by the Church. He is called to be a prophet and a priest. But the ministry has a prophetic and priestly character only because the Church already possesses it. For purposes of order and convenience these functions are normally exercised by special organs. But there is no hard and fast line which divides ministers and laity into fixed and rigid orders. The Church possesses in its own divinely given and inalienable resources the means, as it has the right, to exercise these functions apart from these organs. The minister may rightly rely on Divine grace for the fulfilment of his vocation; and since he leads a separated life, wholly consecrated to his sacred task, he is equipped with special grace for that purpose. But this grace is in no way different in kind from that which any worker in the Church may confidently claim. It is no mysterious spiritual essence with which he is once for all inoculated at his ordination.

It is just the Divine help constantly vouchsafed and adequate to every need: 'As thy day, so shall thy strength be.'

While I deprecate the tendency to pit one form of worship or means of grace against another, I recognize the place of the two sacraments in the life of the Church. But I cannot concede the dominant position often claimed for them. I am profoundly impressed with the difficulties which surround the New Testament references. The problems of exegesis and of lower, higher, and historical criticism present a tangled thicket through which we must cut our way to what truth there may be at the centre. Can matters so vital as is asserted have been left by God in such obscurity and uncertainty? Moreover the sacraments were just the features in Christian worship to which non-Christian interpretations and accretions would most readily be attached. Yet so many precious associations have gathered around the Holy Communion, and experience has so demonstrated its spiritual value, that we may justly accord it an honoured place in our worship.

If the Incarnation was intended to counterwork physical corruption and death by inoculating our flesh and blood with a divine immortal principle, then the Eucharist might be interpreted as an extension of the Incarnation, effecting in the individual what the Incarnation effected for the race. Since the Church is the body of Christ we might speak of it as an extension of the Incarnation, but the term is inapplicable to the Eucharist. We joyfully recognize the real presence of Christ in the Sacrament of Holy Communion. For He is both the Giver and the gift. It is His pierced hands which break for us the bread of life. It is Himself that He gives to the believing soul. But His presence is in the Sacrament as a whole, not localized in the elements, to which it would be better that the term 'Sacrament' should not be applied. If this is recognized, there would in itself be no objection from a strictly Protestant point of view to taking the elements from the Lord's table to the sick. But when it is believed that the real presence is localized in the elements, and abides there even when the congregation of the faithful has dispersed, it is not illogical to say that Christ, actually present in the elements, may be, and indeed ought to be, adored. It is this which constitutes the peril of continuous reservation. But the real presence must be more spiritually interpreted, and it ought not to be regarded as different in kind from that which the Christian experiences in prayer and other acts of devotion. I do not deny that the Eucharist has its own specific value. But this is not to be found in any change which takes place in the elements themselves.

In our Lambeth discussions the question of the relations between the State and the re-united Church was not wholly ignored, but we felt that there was no need to deal explicity with it at this stage. It was understood that if Reunion with the Free Churches could be effected, the Establishment would not be permitted to stand in the way. Moreover, it was quite possible that, independently of any action on our part, the question might be taken up and settled. It was obviously better that disestablishment, if it came, should come from within; or that it should come in the course of political development rather than religious controversy. The happier relations which exist between the Church of England and the Free Churches are so precious an asset to the religious forces of the country that we might rightly hesitate to embitter them by precipitate action, when with patience our ideals might be realized, perhaps by common consent, perhaps on political rather than on ecclesiastical initiative. It is to me quite incredible that the Free Churches would consent to form part of an established Church. There I might leave it, were it not that the whole question has suddenly come to the front as a consequence of the rejection by the House of Commons of the Deposited Prayer Book.

It is part of our Christian duty to render the State our own unstinted service and loyal obedience where this does not clash with our highest loyalty. We must render to Caesar the things that are Caesar's. But there is a realm where Caesar's writ does not run, a sphere which he has no right to invade. There is and can be only one Head of the Church. The prerogatives of the ministry may have their importance; but the crown rights of the Redeemer are far more sacred to me than the rights of any ministry; they touch me to the quick. But what is the present position? The Church suffers the indignity of having by its constitution a secular monarch as its official head. He may be a Christian neither in belief nor practice. Charles II and George IV have stood at the head of the national Church. And if we put this indignity on the Church, we put the indignity on our sovereign of forcing him to belong to a particular Church and to different Churches in different parts of our island. He cannot freely choose the communion to which he would belong; nor can he refrain from belonging to any if his personal convictions are out of harmony with Christianity. We may even compel him to violate his conscience as the price of accepting his crown. Nor can the Church be free to take unflinchingly the Christian line since it is fettered even though it is not paralysed, by its entangling alliance with the State. No Church can do its work aright unless it possesses complete spiritual autonomy. It cannot allow the secular power to determine its beliefs, its organization or the form of its worship. But if a Church has secured autonomy, it ought not to seek to make the best of both worlds by combining it with any secular alliance conferring prerogative and prestige. It is to be trusted that all the Churches may become more Christian. This will create a spirit of love, which will make it intolerable to any established Church to remain in a position of privilege in relation to the State which differentiates it from other Churches.

Our Anglican friends may not always do justice to our motives in desiring the reform of their Church. But the Church of England alike by its magnitude, its social status, its State connexion, inevitably stands as the typical expression of Christianity to our fellow-countrymen. It is a matter of deep concern to us that the representation of our religion should be as worthy as possible. We are convinced that the Establishment hinders this. We sincerely believe that the Anglican Church will never be free to do its best work until it has been emancipated from State control.

There are Anglicans and Free Churchmen who will assent to this; but who desire what is called a State recognition of Christianity. But are we to accept for Christianity what we refuse for an individual Church? No religion ought to permit itself to accept the position of being the State-favoured religion. All the Churches will, as the Spirit of Christ comes to control them, refuse to accept any privilege or prestige from the State which is not equally accorded to all other forms of religion or negations of religion. The State ought to be colour-blind to all religious differences. Citizenship is the only status which it can properly recognize. We ought not to place our fellow-citizens in an invidious position, or impose participation in sacred acts which for them can only be conventional, formal, and insincere. Nor can a religion consistently seek to impose its own specific beliefs on the community. The conscience of the agnostic should be as sacred to us as our own. We are simply entitled to claim the benevolent attitude of the State to our philanthropic work and our attempts to elevate the morality of the people. To the plea, which is sometimes urged, that the State preserves freedom of thought and impartiality as between contending parties in the Church better than the Church itself would do, we can only say that, if true, this is a distressing confession of our imperfection, but that the end does not justify the means.

I pass on to the Roman problem. In his recent encyclical the Pope has put his foot heavily on all projects of Reunion which do not start with submission to the Roman Church as the one and only Church of Christ on earth.[1] This is his comment on Malines, and his answer to Lambeth and Lausanne. It is clear that no Church with any self-respect can think of Reunion on such terms. One could wish that those Anglicans who have looked hopefully to Rome would recognize that, however earnestly some Romans have desired to heal the schism, Rome itself has taken up an attitude and laid down conditions of Reunion such as the English Church cannot possibly accept. Nor could they hope to carry with them the very large body of their fellow-Anglicans who, without being in any sense extremists, will firmly repudiate not simply the Roman claims, but a large mass of the dogmas and practices of the Roman Church, even though shared by the Orthodox Church. In view of Rome's immovable attitude, we may anticipate that the Church of England will abandon all futile approaches to a communion which in arrogant self-confidence claims to be the only true Church, and will readmit those who have separated from her only on their unreserved submission.

It is curious that attention should be concentrated so much on Rome and directed much less to the East. If it were a question of Patriarchates simply it would be natural for the English Church to look toward Rome, of which Church it formed a part till the Reformation, centuries after the schism between East and West. And if geography is to determine ecclesiastical allegiance—though if there is only one true Church geography is irrelevant—and if Britain is too insignificant to have its own Patriarchate, then an Italian Bishop might be suffered to lord it over an English Church. But if I came to the conclusion that the Free Churches were no part of the true Church and that even the Anglican Church was

---

[1] Encyclical Letter (*Mortalium Animos*) of Pius XI, 6th January 1928. See *Documents on Christian Unity*, ed. G. K. A. Bell, Second Series, pp. 51–63.—Ed.

not sufficiently 'Catholic' to justify my allegiance, because its orders were too uncertain, or because it was too deeply infected with Protestant and Modernist heresy, I should feel much more strongly drawn to the East than to Rome. The East has not been manoeuvred into a claim similar to that made by Pius IX at the Vatican Council. Nor has it anything corresponding to Papal supremacy. And while its assertion that there is only one Church, and that the Eastern Orthodox Church, is unflinching, yet its doctrine of 'Economy' enables it to go a long way toward recognizing in practice what its theory could compel it to disown. Rome has no higher credentials than the East, nor has it anything really to offer which the East does not possess.

That Rome will for long exercise her authority over backward races and semi-civilized communities is not unlikely. And among more highly cultured peoples she will retain or attract many by her aesthetic appeal, and many because she offers them a refuge from their doubts and takes over all responsibility for them. There are those who by their very temperament are drawn irresistibly to Rome. Antiquity, continuity, authority, infallibility—claims so proud and so confident exercise a singular fascination on many susceptible souls. The pomp of her services, her wealth of devotions, legitimate and illegitimate, contrast with what they feel to be the bare and bleak austerity of the Protestant forms of worship. But all that the 'Catholic', wavering between Rome and the East, could wisely demand would be provided as well by the East, without the Papal infallibility which strategically strong in appearance, must prove in the long run a fatal entanglement. For now the whole Roman position is staked on the truth of this dogma. But it is suspended by a chain of hypotheses of which very few are raised above a narrow margin of probability, while several are improbable in the last degree. If Matthew 16^{18} is authentic; and if by the 'rock' Peter is intended; and if the passage implies the infallibility of Peter; and if Peter ever resided in Rome; and if residing there he was its Bishop; and if he passed on his prerogatives to later Bishops of Rome; and if he did not pass them on to the Bishops in other places where he resided; if indeed there was any monarchical episcopate in Rome till decades after his time; and if the explicit utterances of Jesus did not forbid such a claim; and if it were not incompatible with much in the New Testament record—then and only then could one concede the Roman claim.

And of what value is the dogma after all? There is a strategic value in a claim which when stated in general terms can be made impressive, attractive, and commanding, but which leaves avenues of escape when it becomes inconvenient to press it. It is at least very effective window-dressing. But when an authoritative statement was needed why has the infallible oracle been so often silent? I have no wish to rob Peter to pay Paul—Peter indeed cannot so well afford it—but I am certainly not going to rob Paul to pay Peter.

If, inspired by a new and sweet humility and a regard for the results of unfettered exegesis and historical research, Rome should renounce her claims to supremacy, her boast of infallibility; if she would revoke all her profane anathemas, repent before the world of her ghastly record of atrocious persecution, and undertake a drastic reform from within, how gladly we should welcome such a triumph of divine grace! But divine grace does not act without the co-operation of the human will; and the will for so splendid a recantation, or indeed any recognition that she owes it to humanity, is, we must judge, entirely absent.

But there is another consideration of vital importance. We think far too exclusively in terms of Europe and the Near East, and of the centuries which lie behind us. Our vision is too contracted alike in time and space. History is still quite young. The Church is slowly emerging from its childhood, slowing escaping from those lower pagan elements which it inevitably absorbed in its early period. The centre of gravity has decisively shifted. The Western Church has meant for us the European Church east of Russia and Greece. But the New World has come in to redress the balance of the Old. We must think in terms of the Western continents, of our dominions beyond the seas, of the great field of missionary enterprise. With this world-wide outlook we can appraise with a juster sense of proportion the claims alike of Rome and the Eastern Orthodox Church. Our eyes must be turned to the future rather than the past. The East is at present paralysed for progress by its immovable attachment to the Seven Councils. Rome is fatally hampered by its claim to infallibility. Both contain elements which Protestantism, while it remains Protestant, cannot possibly accept. Such are the doctrine of the infallibility of the Church and in particular of the dogmatic decrees of the Councils, the invocation of the Virgin and the saints, the change at the moment of consecration of the bread and wine into the actual body and blood of Christ, the adoration of this Eucharistic body and blood with the same worship as is paid to the Trinity, the offering up in the Eucharist of the body of Christ for the quick and the dead, the necessity of confession to a priest and priestly absolution, apostolic succession, the vital necessity of the episcopate to the existence of the Church, the demand that Scripture must be interpreted in accordance with ecclesiastical tradition. Our Protestant interpretation of Scripture must be scientific, not governed by ecclesiastical pronouncements old or new, not anxiously adjusted to tradition or controlled by the exegesis of the Fathers. We cannot surrender our right of private judgement. This right must indeed be earned before it is exercised. We desire a private judgement freely, consciously, and continuously exercised, not a judgement drugged and dragooned by autocratic authority. Rome must increasingly lose those who give its due rights to reason and prize freedom of thought. Much on which 'Catholics' lay stress will not survive as truer and loftier thoughts of God and religion prevail. The God we worship is not an ecclesiastical pedant or martinet. Our theology is dropping its crudities. I will not speak of modernism. It is a term so elastic and so ambiguous that we should give it a prolonged holiday. But this at least I will say, that those who combine a modern outlook with loyalty to the vital principles of the Gospel, are the intellectual salt of an ecclesiastical body which, without it, might quickly lapse into bigotry, obscurantism, and superstition.

Our own deepest trouble is not obscurantism but anaemia, the thinness and poorness of spiritual life. In the records of the early Church we are impressed by the radiant joy, the infectious enthusiasm, the glowing hope, the ardent affection of those early days. Can we match that sense of liberation, that intoxicating rapture, that deep central bliss? The problem is not simply that of making Christians, but of making Christians of the best and highest type. And for this the loftiest morality is not enough. Religion is not just morality touched with emotion. It is the most tremendous force we know. When it bursts into the life in all its explosive energy the fountains of the great deep are broken up. Or it may steal into the life as the dawn into the world and, without crisis, brighten to the perfect day. But it is tragic when the light at noonday is only a stereotyped dawn. Far too many

Christians seem as if they had been vaccinated against any profound experience of religion by too weak an inoculation. If religion is anything in our lives it ought to be everything; not in the sense that it shuts out all other interests, but that it supplies the underlying harmony to every melody of life. But we search too little among the roots of our religion; we live too much on the shallow crust, too little at the fiery centre. Our endless and sometimes fussy and futile activities call us from the still brooding and the mystical fellowship in which the mind gains depth and lucidity of vision, while the tired and fretful spirit finds strength, refreshment, and peace.

Deeper than all else is our right adjustment to God. To love Him with every faculty of our being, strained to the utmost tension, must always be our Christian ideal. And we cannot love Him as we should if He remains to us vague, impenetrable, and remote. We need a vivid realization of Him. To know God for ourselves, that is eternal life. He has not left Himself without a witness. Dark and enigmatic in Nature; less dimly manifested in history as we view it on the large scale; His voice is heard in the judgements of conscience, we meet Him as we thread the labyrinth of our own heart. He chose Israel as the sphere of a unique self-disclosure, made first through the history of a whole people, and then through the experience of elect personalities—prophet, psalmist and sage. In Jesus this reached the consummation toward which from the outset the whole movement had been steadily guided. And while He taught us about God, our deepest knowledge of Him comes as we steep ourselves in the Gospels, and the personality of Jesus disengages itself from the record. For He is the manifestation in human character, personality, and action of God Himself. He is God's self-translation from the speech of eternity into the speech of time. Our religion is inseparably associated with Him; were He withdrawn from it, it would wither at the root. Ours is the religion of the Incarnation and the Passion, of the Cradle and the Cross. To serve Him with utter devotion is our supreme privilege, to confess Him before men is the loftiest dignity accorded to human lips.

Our feeble powers cannot compass the task of re-translating God from this limited speech of time into the mighty language of His own eternity. Yet our knowledge of Him has been immeasurably enriched by His self-revelation in Jesus. His essence is pure spirit, His moral nature boundless and unfathomable love. But His love is one with His holiness, and should inspire man, not with affectionate familiarity, but with an answering love penetrated by the deepest reverence. We must never forget the infinite distance which separates the highest of created beings from its Creator, or lose from our thought of God the awe-struck sense of His majesty, His power, His wisdom, and His holiness. When the fear of God has vanished we have lost that antiseptic element which can alone preserve our religion from corruption. I welcome the tendency to emphasize once more this conception of God and redress a balance which had been dangerously disturbed.

But Jesus did more than disclose God to us. Sin had poisoned our relations with God, darkened and confused our moral judgement, stained and blunted our conscience, paralysed our will, and burdened us with a sense of guilt. Jesus brought us the tidings of God's love and met all the moral demands of the situation. He knew our life from the inside, learnt sympathy with us by submitting to the awful strain of temptation, took on Himself the shame and burden of our sin, drank to the dregs the cup which could not pass from Him, tasting to the full every flavour in its mingled bitterness. So He reconciled man to God. The tiny band of disciples rallied by His resurrection and equipped by Pentecost, formed a society filled with Divine enthusiasm. They made their appeal to Israel and then carried the glad tidings to the Gentiles. The message of the Cross was an insuperable obstacle to the Jews, sheer lunacy to the Greeks, yet it turned the world upside down.

Of this the New Testament gives us the record and the interpretation, telling us also how the ascended Lord carried on His work through His Holy Spirit, inspiring the Church and its ministry. The Old Testament is the necessary preliminary to the New, enabling us to trace this unique movement of revelation from its beginning to its completion. The Bible is thus an indispensable means of grace, open and accessible to all Christians to be studied in the light of the best scholarship, to be withheld even from the humblest, only to their irretrievable and inexcusable loss. No public ministry of the Word, no private prayer, no sacramental grace can take its place in the cultivation of the spiritual life, precious in their own way as each of these may be. One of the surest signs of decadence in the Church, as it is one of its most efficient causes, is the neglect of the classical documents of our religion.

As Protestants we stand for the priesthood of all believers, for the right of private judgement, for the unrestricted use of Scripture, for the freedom of the Christian man, for the direct access of the soul to God. We repudiate the Papal supremacy, all human infallibility, whether of Church, Council or Pope, all worship, however defined, of angel, Virgin or saints, all change in the Eucharistic elements. We claim no monopoly of truth; we do not deny that other communions are true branches of the Church of Christ, but we dare not question our divine vocation. We recognize that some forms of Christianity may appeal to certain types of personality and temperament better than our own. We realize that our Church must have a message for our own age and yet be loyal to the faith once for all delivered to the saints. We humbly trust that the world, wistfully seeking for the truth, may discern in our hands the print of the nails, and hear in our message the authentic utterance of our Crucified Lord.

APPENDIX
SELECT BIBLIOGRAPHY
of Dr A. S. Peake's Printed Works

The following bibliography is necessarily incomplete. Some of the material is elusive, for sometimes review articles are unsigned; also the amount of material is so vast that time has not allowed for complete search, and in any case space would forbid the printing of a complete record, if such could be made. Selection has therefore been necessary.

This bibliography takes no account of the enormous number of Reviews to be found in the pages of the *Holborn Review* (during the years 1919–29); in the *Times Literary Supplement*, some fifty of which fortunately survive amongst the Peake Papers in the Library of Hartley Victoria College, and which, although they bear no printed indication of the writer, bear Peake's written signature, yet probably form only a part of his contribution to that periodical; in the *Primitive Methodist Leader*, to the columns of which Peake contributed regularly from 1907 onward until his death; and in other periodicals. Neither does it indicate his large correspondence.

Nor are all the articles which have been traced recorded here, owing to restrictions of space. Those set down, however, may be regarded as representative, and the following list will serve at least to indicate something of Peake's enormous literary output, and will reveal his deep concern to mediate the truth of Christianity and the results of modern scholarship to the ordinary person.

Abbreviations:
        H.R.: *Holborn Review.*
        P.M.L.: *Primitive Methodist Leader.*
        B.J.R.L.: *Bulletin of John Rylands Library.*

1894
'Thomas Kelly Cheyne' in *Expository Times*, Vol. VI.

1895–6
'Wellhausen and Dr Baxter' in *Expository Times*, Vols. VII–VIII.

1897
A Guide to Biblical Study.

1902
The Epistle to the Hebrews in 'The Century Bible'.

1903
The Epistle to the Colossians in Expositor's Greek Testament, Vol. III.

1904
Articles as below in Hastings' *Dictionary of the Bible:*
Ahaz, Baal, Benjamin, Dan, Dionysia, Ecclesiastes, First Fruits, Issachar, Josiah, Judah, Manasseh, Uncleanness, Vow.
The Problem of Suffering in the Old Testament (Hartley Lecture 1904; re-printed 1952).

1905
The Book of Job in 'The Century Bible'.
(Edited) *Inaugural Lectures delivered by Members of the Faculty of Theology* (1904-5). (University of Manchester.)

1906
Reform in Sunday School Teaching.
Article in Hasting's *Dictionary of Christ and the Gospels:* Immanuel.

1907
(As part-author) 'Messianic Prophecy' in *Lux Hominum: Studies of the Living Christ in the World of Today*, ed. by F. W. Orde Ward.
Articles in *P.M.L.* (a series dealing with scripture texts usually misunderstood and misapplied). Those marked with an asterisk are reprinted in *Plain Thoughts on Great Subjects:*
*'I have trodden the wine-press alone.'
*'Fools shall err elsewhere.'
'A peculiar People.'
*'Not with water only.'
'My Spirit shall not always strive.'
'How art thou fallen from Heaven.'
*'Ye search the Scriptures.'
*'Christ's suffering in our flesh.'
'The heart of the Gospel.'
'The Presentation of Jesus in the Gospel of Mark.'

1908
The Religion of Israel.
Christianity: Its Nature and Truth.
The Christian Race.
Election and Service.
Faded Myths.

Articles in the *P.M.L.*:
'The Incarnation and Recent Criticism.'
'The New Gospel Fragment.'
'Studies in the Inner Life of Jesus' (two arts.).

1909

A Critical Introduction to the New Testament.
Article in Hastings' *Encyclopaedia of Religion and Ethics*: Basilides.
Articles in the *P.M.L.*:
'The Faith of the Prophets' (three arts.).
'The Place of the Evangel in the Preaching of Today.'
'The Bible in the Light of Modern Research.'
'The Son of Perdition.'
'Lord, is it I?'
'Studies in Mystical Religion' (two arts.).
'The Christian Doctrine of God.'

1910

Article in Hastings' *Encyclopaedia of Religion and Ethics*: Cerinthus.
'Some recent New Testament Literature' in *H.R.*
Heroes and Martyrs of Faith.
The Book of Jeremiah (Vol. I) in 'The Century Bible'.
Articles in the *P.M.L.*:
'The Gospels as Historical Documents.'
'The Person and Place of Jesus Christ.'
'Telling the Truth as a Fine Art.'
'The Revised Version with fuller References.'
'The Perennial Fountain and the Broken Cistern.'
'The Jungle of Jordan.'
'The Inspiration of Prophecy.'
'The Tercentenary of the Authorized Version.'

1911

'Recent Literature on the New Testament' in *H.R.*
'Dr Moffatt's Introduction to the New Testament' in *H.R.*
Articles in the *P.M.L.*:
'The Tercentenary of the Authorized Version.'
'The English Church in the Nineteenth Century.'
'The Transcendance of God and the Authority of the Church.'

1912

The Book of Jeremiah (2 vols.) in 'The Century Bible'.
'Some recent work in Anthropology and Religion' in *H.R.*

Articles in the *P.M.L.*:
'Time in the Light of Eternity.'
'Robertson Smith (two arts.).'
'Principal A. M. Fairbairn' in *The Expositor*.

1913
'Some Recent Literature on the New Testament' in *H.R.*
Articles in Hastings' *Dictionary of Christ and the Gospels*:
   Mockery.
   Parable of the Talents.
The Bible: its Origin, its Significance and Abiding Worth.
Article in the *P.M.L.*:
   'Comparative Religion and Christian Missions.'

1914
'Bibliographical Notes for Students of the Old and New Testaments' in *B.J.R.L.*
Article in the *P.M.L*:
   'Paul and other Theologians.'
'Professor S. R. Driver' in *The Expositor*.

1915
Articles in Hastings' *Dictionary of the Apostolic Church:*
   Cainites.
   Jude.
   The Lord's Brother.
   Epistle of Jude.
'The Life of Dr Fairbairn' in *H.R.*
The History of German Theology during the Nineteenth Century.

1917
'A Record of Professor J. H. Moulton's work with some explanation of its Significance in *James Hope Moulton, 1863–1917*.'
'The Quintessence of Paulinism' in *B.J.R.L.*, Vol. IV.

1918
Prisoners of Hope: The Problem of the Conscientious Objector.

1919
'In Memoriam: H. E. Kendall and J. Day Thompson' in *H.R.*
Peake's Commentary on the Bible (edited).
The following articles are written by A. S. Peake:
   The Development of Old Testament Literature.
   The Chronology of the Old Testament.

Genesis.
The Poetical and Wisdom Literature.
The Prophetic Literature.
Isaiah 1–39.
Jonah.
Organization, Church Meetings, Discipline, Social and Ethical Problems.
The Pauline Epistles.
1 Corinthians.
General Bibliographies.
(Part-author) 'The Person of Christ in the Revelation of John' in *Mansfield College Essays presented to A. M. Fairbairn*.
The Revelation of John (Hartley Lecture).

1920

Articles in the *P.M.L.*:
'Methodist Union: The Doctrinal Statement.'
'Methodist Union: Why remain separate?'
'In League with the stones of the field' in *Expository Times*, Vol. XXXIV.
'Some recent New Testament Literature' (three arts.). in *H.R.*
'The Roots of Jewish Prophecy and Jewish Apocalyptic' in *B.J.R.L.*, Vol. VII.
'Dr Sanday' in *The Expositor*.

1921

Articles in the *P.M.L.*:
'Methodist Union: The Ministerial Office Defined.'
'The Victorian Attitude.'
'The New Situation.'
'The Army and Religion.'
'The Average Soldier.'

1922

The Nature of Scripture.
Articles in *P.M.L.*:
'The Indictment of the Churches.' (five arts.).
'Christianity and War.'
'How the War raised new Problems in Theology.'
'The War and German Theology.'
'Commending Christianity.'
'A Standard Christianity.'
'Methodist Union Opposition: Indictment of the manifesto.'

'The Re-Union of Christendom.' (Notes of an address given at the Unity Meeting of the Wesleyan Conference at Sheffield on 25th July.)
'Methodist Union Proposals: The Ministerial Session.'

1923
Brotherhood in the Old Testament.
Article in *P.M.L.*:
'The Old Testament in the Sunday School.'

1924
'The Messiah and the Son of Man' in *B.J.R.L.*, Vol. VIII.
Articles in *P.M.L.*:
'Methodist Union and Doctrinal Standards.'
'Methodist Union and the Sacraments.'
'The Methodist Pulpit and Modern Thought.'
'Christ's Unsearchable Riches' (a sermon).
'Methodist Union: Reasons for acceptance of the Scheme.'

1925
The Life of Sir William P. Hartley.
Theology and Classical Scholarship in *H.R.*
(As co-Editor) *An Outline of Christianity* (five vols.).
Chapters by A. S. Peake on:
'The Preparation for Christianity in Israel' (Vol. I).
'The New Testament Assembled' (Vol. I).
'The Genius of Methodism.' (Vol. III).
'The Criticism of the Old Testament' (Vol. IV).
(Editor) *The People and the Book.*
Chapter on 'The Religion of Israel from David to the Return from Exile'.

1926
'Some Recent Biblical Literature' in *H.R.*
'Sir William Robertson Nicoll' in *H.R.*
'Introduction and a Bibliography for English Readers' in *Introduction to the Old Testament;* E. Sellin, trans. by W. Montgomery.
Articles in a *New Standard Bible Dictionary* (ed. by M. W. Jacobus, E. E. Nourse, and A. C. Zenos): Isaiah: The Religion of Israel: Jeremiah.

1927
'Some Notes on Recent Biblical Literature' in *H.R.*
'Elijah and Jezebel' in *B.J.R.L.*, Vol. XI.

'Commentaries on the Old and New Testaments' (four arts.) in *Expository Times*, Vol. XXXIX.

1928

'Paul the Apostle: his Personality and Achievement' in *B.J.R.L.*, Vol. XII.
'Recent Developments in Old Testament Criticism.' in *B.J.R.L.*, Vol. XII.
'Pray for the Peace of Jerusalem.' Presidential Address of the National Free Church Council, 1928, *P.M.L.*, 15th March. Reprinted in *Plain Thoughts on Great Subjects* (n.d.) under the title 'The Re-union of the Churches'.

1929

'Paul and the Jewish Christians' in *B.J.R.L.*, Vol. XIII.

1931

The Servant of Yahweh: Three Lectures delivered at King's College, London, during 1926, *together with The Rylands Lecture on Old Testament and New Testament subjects.* Prefaced with Memorial Tribute by Dr Henry Guppy, Librarian of the John Rylands Library, Manchester.

BOOKS ON DR PEAKE

Arthur Samuel Peake, by Leslie S. Peake (1930).
Plain Thoughts on Great Subjects, ed. L. S. Peake (n.d.).
Recollections and Appreciations, ed. W. F. Howard (1938).

www.ingramcontent.com/pod-product-compliance
Lightning Source LLC
Chambersburg PA
CBHW051938160426
43198CB00013B/2202